THE
LANGUAGE
OF
WATER

THE
LANGUAGE
OF
WATER

A Woman's Life
With Systemic Lupus
Erythematosus

JUDE CLARKE

thistledown press

Canadian Cataloguing in Publication Data

Clarke, Jude.
The language of water

ISBN 1-894345-44-4
I. Clarke, Jude–Health. 2. Systemic lupus erythematosus–
Patients–Biography. 3. Artists, Canadian–Biography. I. Title.
RC924.5.L85C52 2002   362.1'9677   C2002-910325-8

Cover painting detail, *Breakthrough*, by Jude Clarke
Cover and book design by Jackie Forrie
Typeset by Thistledown Press Ltd.
Printed and bound in Canada

Poems and song lyrics by John Lent

Thistledown Press Ltd.
633 Main Street
Saskatoon, Saskatchewan
S7H 0J8

Thistledown Press gratefully acknowledges the financial assistance of the
Canada Council for the Arts, the Saskatchewan Arts Board, and the
Government of Canada through the Book Publishing Industry
Development Program for its publishing program.

ACKNOWLEDGEMENTS

I want to thank everybody in the two, huge, warm families that John and I share, for all their support. I would especially like to thank Norman and Jean McQuay who read my manuscript as it was being written, as well as Alison McQuay, for their singular interest in this project. I have been under the care of several remarkable doctors in Canada, France, England and Scotland over the years and wish to thank them here for their expertise and compassion. In order to protect their privacy, the names of physicians and others have been changed in this book.

I am grateful to Simone Vauthier who went over the France sections. Thank you to Seán Virgo who inspired me to re-envision the manuscript, and who edited it with warmth, gentility and an eagle eye.

My thanks to Rhonda Cameron, Wendy Carter, Chris Francis, Liz Hamilton, Ronnie de Langon, Debbie Lent, Carole Reid and Linda McConnell. Thank you to Franny, my quiet, wise sister who never lets me give up and whose empathy is felt by all who know her. Thank you doesn't begin to express what I want to say to my husband, John, who has travelled this strange, unknown road with me, always.

CONTENTS

ILLUSTRATIONS

to John,
my heart's desire

to my mother, and in memory of my father

to Len, Franny, and Joe

Spring, 1999

TWENTY-TWO YEARS AGO, at the age of twenty-one, I was diagnosed with Systemic Lupus Erythematosus. Derived from the Latin word meaning "wolf", and named so because of the ravaging effect it has on the body, lupus is a chronic, autoimmune, inflammatory, connective-tissue disease. This means my immune system is confused, doesn't understand what it's supposed to do. It turns against itself and attacks its own healthy tissues and organs, causing minor and major physical manifestations, and consequently great emotional turmoil. Statistics show this is a disease that primarily affects women in their child-bearing years.

Some twelve years ago, I began to think about documenting my personal experience of living with lupus. Initially, because I'm a visual artist, I thought I would do a series of paintings which would develop a portrait of the disease from a psychological point of view. Each time I went into a serious disease-active period (for me, this means kidney involvement), I would think about the project. I started making sketches and jotting down ideas. I would be enthusiastic until I was through the active period which will, hereafter, be referred to as a "flare". As soon as I was in remission, I would abandon the project. I was well. I didn't want to dwell on the disease or the flare a moment longer. It was bad enough living it; I didn't want to relive it again, in my art. So I would inevitably put away my notes and drawings and gratefully get back to living my life.

My kidney function was affected by the lupus for the fourth time, a year and a half ago. As usual, this flare consumed a year of my life from beginning to remission. Once again, it was a time for introspection, a time to try and make sense of this immune disorder. I realized the presence or fact of this disease had influenced every decision I'd ever made, either consciously or unconsciously. I understood the lupus had a great deal to do with what my life had become and who I was. More surprisingly, I also realized that who I am, innately, has influenced the effect of this disease on my life more than I would ever have thought possible. This was a revelation.

So many times over the years, I felt I was free falling. My immune system was out of control and nothing could prevent it from doing what it was going to do. This, of course, is essentially true. However, I know now that my spirit had been just as strong and intrinsically determined to triumph as the disease seemed to have been. At twenty-one, I didn't know this. I was terrified and overwhelmed with what was happening inside my body, and tense and afraid of what was to come. Not even the doctors could tell me the course my disease would take.

One day in January 1999, four months after I had completely recovered from this fourth kidney flare, I went into my studio and without much forethought put together a small collage representing a wildfire and a wolf. I taped it onto my studio wall. I typed out a prose piece I'd written years ago and taped it beside the collage. The next day, I made another collage. Suddenly, I had two images, and surprisingly, the beginning of a narrative. In time, the narrative took on a life of its own. Every day, I would paint a little and then write a little more. Soon, I had set aside my paints and was just writing. I thought of the writing as a series of small paintings or vignettes which when strung together, would make a large, whole work. I didn't stop to think about what I was doing; I just followed my instincts. It was exhilarating. I couldn't wait to sit down at the computer every morning and see what would come out. The narrative text didn't arrive in a linear way; a vignette would appear in my head and I'd start typing. Eventually, these vignettes began to fall into an order and I found myself interspersing them with sections of straight narrative — chronological facts and details. My intention to produce a series of paintings had transformed into a written document. I could begin to sense a strange kind of wholeness to the narrative, a unity not necessarily provided by the chronological. I understood this kind of unity or wholeness from my own experiments in abstraction in painting. And yet, I sensed, too, that I needed a chronological understructure in order to tell the story of the disease's progress.

There were specific childhood memories that seemed important, integral and essential to the whole story. I felt their inclusion would set up the full, human context for my becoming ill. I wanted to portray my relationship with my brothers and sister and my parents in this childhood context, too. I wanted to write about being a young woman, my marriage, my career as an artist, all the things I did or didn't do as I struggled with this disease.

At the beginning, I suppose I was writing for myself and my family, but something I had read when I was thirty-two and had just emerged from the worst period of my illness had stayed with me all these years. It was an article in a newspaper about a young woman. Her brother had been interviewed and he explained how his vibrant, sociable sister had changed over the course of a few years into a tired, reclusive, inexplicably ill-seeming person. She had committed suicide at the age of twenty-three. When an autopsy was performed, it was discovered she had undiagnosed systemic lupus.

In the face of that article, I wanted people to know about the life of a person who has lupus. I wanted to acknowledge the great psychological trauma of the diagnosis and the further trauma of living day-to-day with the capricious manifestations of this disease. That young woman must have felt so ill and alone. She never knew she had a clinical disease, that there was an explanation for how she was feeling. I can only imagine what her life was and what it could have been. I find it hard to think about her.

My hope is that this piece will help someone else diagnosed with lupus to feel less alone and less fearful. If one young woman, newly diagnosed, reads this and it encourages her to look within herself for her own strength, I'll feel it's been a worthwhile effort. I know there are no shortcuts to the place I am now. Even though each person diagnosed with lupus has to find his or her own understanding of this disease in his or her own time, I wish I could have read something like this when I first became ill. I think it would have helped me to believe I could have, not just a life, but a *good* life.

Figure 1
Breakthrough, 1989
Watercolour

Figure 2
Earth Ascending #3, 1993
Watercolour

November, 2001

IT IS AN ORDINARY ACT, this getting into the car and driving across the prairie with John, but every detail of it seems extraordinary to me. Five months ago I couldn't have imagined I'd be making this trip. Neither John nor I would have believed the flare was really over, that we could plan something like this. But here we are, driving down a gravel side road, an hour east of Brooks, Alberta, on our way to Eastend to stay in the Wallace Stegner house. John is going to use the time to write and I'll be meeting with Seán, the person who will be editing this book. Right now I'm gazing through the side window at the land whizzing by, mesmerized by its seemingly endless wide-openness.

This landscape is a minimalist's dream. Blue sky. Brown earth. Perfectly flat horizon line between. Land held secure by a great, cerulean sky. But sky is only air. It can't really hold anything down.

A slight feeling of vertigo washes over me. There are no sides to this landscape. I'm used to hills and mountains cradling the town where I live and I'm used to looking at a curved horizon line. The morning sun is slanting through the front window, but with sunscreen on and my visor pulled low, I am safe from its ultraviolet rays. Looking out from under all this protection, the light is still bright and when I close my eyes, a pulsing red wall fills my vision.

I hope the car doesn't break down out here. I couldn't even step outside. There's no shade. A certain death trap for me.

But even these thoughts can't spoil my mood. John and I have been joking back and forth, giving each other a hard time as usual, frequently including Finnegan in the fun. She's curled like a cashew nut, nose to butt, on a pillow in her wicker basket in the back seat. She's got her "I'm Finnegan, and I like it like that" expression on her face. This Lhasa Apso loves to travel. She loves the open road.

This is an opportunity. I am returning to the landscape where it all began, where my illness was first named. The prairie before me is a blank canvas on which I can lay down the memory-lines of that time. I am in the landscape. It is possible that I will find a new perspective, and, even, that I will begin to draw new lines.

~~~~

There's a wolf running ahead of the flames through the dry prairie grass. Eyes wildly scanning the horizon, she searches for a safe haven. A body of water. But there is no water. Her heart beats hard, seems an alien weight in her chest. There is smoke. She can't breathe. Ravenous and lost, made crazy by fear, she turns on herself, splices her own skin, clamps down hard on her own heart.

~~~~

I grew up in a small town in the interior of British Columbia, a place reminiscent of Dylan Thomas's pastoral Wales. Vernon sits in a valley called the Okanagan, edged by three lakes and hills, beyond which rise the great, blue humps of the Monashee Mountains. There's a brief interlude in the spring when the grey-brown grasses of winter turn viridian and the hills are flecked through with the brilliance of yellow balsam root ("sunflowers" to the locals) and blue lupins. Soon, the fruit trees burst into bloom: pure white petals through all the variables of pink. The dark burgundy leaves of crabapple trees and Japanese maples anchor the composition and the distant mountains give depth to the pastoral. The fragrance of lilac fills the air and in one day it seems, hundreds of buttercups, crocuses and chiono-doxa burst into bloom from tiny green buds.

In late June, the hills change again, slowly baking to a dull gold in the dry heat of an Okanagan summer. Then it's a landscape of sharp contrast, a natural semi-desert —

cactus country — broken only by lakewater and patches of heavily irrigated orchards. In town, the air shimmers off the pavement and the streets are mostly deserted on the weekends: everyone heads for the lake or finds respite in their gardens near the cooling sweep of watering sprinklers.

~~~~

My father had made the best investment of his life a couple of years before he met my mother. He bought a lakefront lot with a two-room cabin on it for eight hundred dollars on Kalamalka Lake. I've been told his plan was to remain a bachelor; he'd work for his father, play tennis and throw great "lake" parties. He and a buddy had even built a sailboat out there, a boat which on the day of its big launch hovered majestically for a full, glorious minute before slowly sinking — the triumphant cheers of my father and his friends turning to groans and then peals of laughter.

Our family lived in this cabin on the lake every summer during my childhood. We moved out there the day after school got out in June, and came back the day before Labour Day, in time for our annual hike to Grey Ditch. These were endless, hot summer days when we rarely left the green and blue and clear-to-the-sandy-bottom water, summer nights with friends sleeping over, trampolines and a treat at the nearby campground every Friday night, rainy days with games and hot chocolate and fires. We had a sailboat — one that floated — with blue and white-striped sails and a translucent blue fibreglass rowboat which we rowed down to the Pumphouse every day to get our drinking water, singing *Row, Row, Row Your Boat* at the top of our lungs.

It was heaven. Idyllic. My own "Fern Hill". I grew up feeling there was always enough room in our house to be whoever it was I thought I wanted to be. Love was a steady heartbeat. It was the strength of that love which drew my family closer together when we were faced with a darker reality, one that was to affect all of our lives, in different ways.

My father was ill in his forties and fifties with manic depression. For as long as I can remember I had felt protective of my father. I remember his depressions, the bewilderment and worry in his eyes, the long sleeps in the middle of the day. His pacing, the wringing of his hands. And yet in the midst of all this, the comfort of his hand on my forehead as he sat with me through yet another of my childhood headaches. His long, craggy face, the tone of his voice as he assured me my pain would soon go away.

After the depressive phase of my father's illness, he would slowly but inevitably spiral up into hyperactivity. Then, he would be charged with energy and ideas for projects. He'd be "taking care of business". I've read that people with manic depression disorder can go on major spending sprees, spending all their money or giving it away. My dad would bring home gifts from the hardware store for my mother. I'll never forget the day (I was about fifteen) Dad came whistling through the front door and presented Mom with a new broom. In his other hand was a second new broom which he gaily handed over to her, too. I can remember the pause as we all registered the oddity of buying two brooms at one time, and then the expression on my mother's face (and his!) as she said, "Reid, don't bring me home one more damn thing from Fisher's Hardware!" That scene pretty well sums up the extent of my father's spending frenzies. It was hard not to laugh at the time and it makes me laugh still.

As a child I absorbed my father's highs and lows through his gestures, his demeanour, his fears not spoken and the ones I imagined were being whispered behind closed doors between him and my mother. I carried all this into adulthood and it laid the foundation for and shaped the ways I would eventually cope with illness myself.

Summer was always Dad's period of grace, when he felt the most well. Even as a child, I must have sensed the absence of wound-up energy or depression in him. We must have all felt this easing of the disease. My memories of those summers are bathed in a singularly golden light.

Summer, 1963 (age 8)

My summertime friend and I are lying face down on the pier looking at the water through cracks in the wood. We've spent the last hour playing "toga fashion": a game that has us strutting up and down the runway (the pier) showing off various creations we've made out of gaudily-coloured beach towels.

Susan suddenly dips her hand into the water and splashes me. I shriek and we're up, cannonballing into the aqua water. The shock of cold water on sun-baked skin. My feet touch the sandy bottom, and pushing hard I propel myself up through water into air. I break the surface gasping, giggling.

We splash our way to shore and giggle louder when Jo-Jo roars, "Get owtta here!" We've just disturbed his "hunting ground"; he's got a glass pickle jar in each hand and is catching crayfish and bullheads in the shallow water under the willow tree. All the caught ones are in a bucket of water on the lawn which he dumps back into the lake at the end of the day, crowing, "I got nine bullheads today! Three more than yesterday! I am the champion!"

Susan and I grab our towels, run up the path to the side of the road, spread them over the hot pavement and lie there on our backs until we are heated through, warm as toast.

Two little girls, faces tipped to the sun, berry-brown skin, hearts opening to a clear blue sky.

We spend the rest of the afternoon at Susan's grandparent's house, sitting side by side at a desk in a cool back bedroom. Two True Love comic books are laid out before us and we're drawing, copying in pencil the faces and curvaceous bodies of two teenage-girls-in-love. We wonder if we'll ever have curves like that or if we'll ever go on a picnic holding the hands of tall, dark-haired boys like the girls in these comics do.

"I'm going to be an artist when I grow up," I say.

"So am I."

"Your drawing is sooo . . . good!"
"So is yours!"

Spring, 1964 (age 9)

I walk home after school, as fast as I can without throwing up, my head pounding. This day, instead of filling a washcloth as I usually do with ice cubes and going to bed with the "throw-up pot" beside me on the floor, I spy my black rubber India ball in a corner of the hallway. I pick it up and go out the back door, down the steps to the best stepping stone on the path. This one is big enough and flat enough for the game. I start bouncing the ball.

"A my name is Annabelle." Leg over ball. "My husband's name is Alfred." Leg over ball. "We live in Armstrong and we sell apples!" Leg over ball. And . . . catch!

"B my name is Betty. My husband's name is Barney. We live in Boston and we sell buttons!"

"C my name is . . . "

I'm at M when I notice my headache is gone. *I did that. I got rid of my own headache.*

I run inside to tell Mom and find out what's for supper.

Fall, 1965 (age 10)

Mom and I have driven down the valley to visit Dad in the hospital. I'm standing looking out the small upstairs window of his room, at some people walking on the sidewalk below. My parents are talking quietly behind me. I'm trying not to cry. I'm holding my body as tightly as possible so that when I turn around, Daddy won't see my tears. Mom must sense this because now she's standing beside me at the window, her arms around me. The tears well up and spill down my face.

"I'm sorry, Daddy. I just want you to get better and come home."

"I know, honey. I'm going to, soon." He looks away. His voice isn't my dad's voice. It sounds unsure and kind of fake, like he got it from somebody else.

Driving home, I can't stop crying. Mom pulls off the highway onto a dirt orchard road and turns off the car. She says, "Just cry it out, honey. Get it all out."

"I don't want to go back there again, Mommy. I don't want to see Daddy again until he comes home."

We are sitting parked amidst apple trees, their leaves crisped and burnt-orange in the sun. We roll the windows down and let in the air, fragrant with ripe apples. In the distance, through the branches, I can see a small triangle of deep blue: the lake.

Winter, 1967 (age 12)

Mom and I are in the kitchen finishing up the supper dishes. For the third time I say, "Are you sure?"

She folds the dishtowel and drapes it over the rod on the stove. "Yes!!! Go!!! I love having time to myself. Peace and quiet for a change. Go out with your friends."

Dad is in the hospital in Kelowna receiving shock treatments. Franny and Len are at university in Vancouver and Joe and I are the only two left at home.

She calls out to my brother in the living room, "Joe, aren't you going out, too?"

"Nah. I think I'll just hang out here. Nothin's happening tonight, anyway."

My sixteen-year-old brother stays home with our mother every weekend this winter while our father is in the hospital.

1968 (age 13)

The Beatles release their 45 with "Hey Jude" on the A-side and "Revolution" on the B. After scores of repeat playing, holed up in the den with the door closed and the volume cranked up as loud as it can be without drawing my mother's attention, I unofficially change my name to Jude. It's way "cooler" than Judy and that dumb song it always reminds me of, "It's Judy's Turn to Cry".

1971-1973 (age 16 – 17)

The last two years of high school go by in a big, happy blur. I put as little effort as possible, without failing, into the subjects I don't care about and live for my literature and art classes. I have three close girlfriends. We drive everywhere on weekend nights when one of us has the use of the family car. We always buy a bit of pot from "the boys" for the weekend, and once in awhile smoke a joint on our school lunch break. This is great for art class but pretty disastrous if I have French. I always sound so stupid anyway, can never get the accent to sound anything remotely French-like, and the grammar paralyses me. The pot makes my comprehension and verbal skills even worse, and then I blush and start laughing.

Once in awhile in the spring, the four of us skip school and head out for an afternoon at the cabin, lying on the pier, baking in the sun and yacking for hours. I just keep my fingers crossed that Dad won't pick this day to come whistling down the path, here to do some odd jobs around the cabin.

We do get a surprise one day though. Traipsing down the path we discover three Rubenesque girls, a few years older than us, tanning, lying stark naked on the pier. In broad daylight.

They invite us to join them.

These girls are three years more worldly than we are. We're sixteen years old and still shy about our bodies, even with each other, and definitely with strangers. We try to make a "cool" escape: "Oh, actually, I just wanted to pick up this . . . rake, for my dad. Thanks, though," and we walk self-consciously, purposely not hurrying, back up the path.

June, 1973 (age 17)

My name is called and now I'm crossing the stage, arm outstretched to shake the hand of the tiny, bird-like woman, "Thank you so much, Mrs. Pitt."

She hands me the scholarship certificate and looks me right in the eye. "Don't thank me, dear. Just work hard, making art."

"I will."

~~~~~

Four girls, seventeen years old, just graduated and giddy, knowing that their lives are about to begin, driving up and down the main street in one of their fathers' cars, smoking. Waving at "the boys"'nonchalantly. Laughing at everything and laughing just as hard at nothing.

But the winter before, one of the girls' fingers turning white, numb with cold against the black leather of the Maverick's steering wheel. She cups her hand under her armpit and the warmth thaws the finger, blue and aching.

July, 1973

My friend David and I are flying to Calgary together. He's continuing on east to Ontario to work, and I'm flying north to Whitehorse to meet up with my sister and her boyfriend. They're working on an OFY (Opportunities for Youth) government grant, running a day camp for native kids. They need someone to teach arts and crafts and I can't wait to fill the role.

Everything is going as planned — my life really is beginning! Things are even better than I had hoped — I meet a boy on the project and have a summer romance.

I return home in August, pack a suitcase full of embroidered shirts and jeans, long flowered skirts and my prize possession — a pair of used black army boots my friends and I found in an army surplus store on a weekend trip to Vancouver. I am going to Nelson to start my first year in the Bachelor of Fine Arts program at Notre Dame University. I hope I'll meet friends quickly — no one else I know from Vernon is going there. Even though I'll be staying in residence, I feel like I'll be on my own! Independent!

This mountain town is perfect — full of musicians, artists, students like me, draft dodgers, people who have "dropped out" from the States, film writers, poets, architects, you name it, Nelson has it. It's alive.

Though I don't begin to know it until the end of this first year, my destiny had arrived a week before me. John had applied from Toronto, where he was finishing his dissertation, to NDU for a position teaching literature and creative writing. He is twenty-five years old and thrilled to have his first real teaching job. The first time I see John, he's walking from the cafeteria across the green lawn and down the stairs into the main administration office. Some new friends and I are playing frisbee on the lawn and I notice this tall lean person with dark beard and hair, balancing a mug of coffee in one hand and a cigarette and book in the other, looking our way and smiling. He has an amazing smile. We all smile back. I assume he is a student. The next time I see him, he walks into the literature class I'm taking, continues on to the front of the room, turns around and says, "Hi everybody. My name's John Lent and I'm your instructor for the year."

You've got to be kidding.

November, 1973

Franny and I are both home from university. We've just been talking to Mom in the living room and are now standing in my old bedroom with the door closed.

"So we'll go down around eleven, okay?"

"Okay."

Franny starts to cry and we reach out for each other.

"It's all right, Franny. Everything's going to be all right."

The next morning, we enter the old brick psychiatric building which is separate from the rest of the hospital. We walk through a lobby that's been turned into a "living room" of sorts. It's dimly lit and we walk past several people slouched in old chairs around the room. There isn't a sound in the room. We turn down another hallway to Dad's room. I follow Franny through the doorway.

"There's my girls! Hi, kids."

Dad is rising from a prone position on the narrow hospital bed. His eyes are the bluest I've ever seen them. There is innocence mixed with a slight questioning, a bewilderment in them. He picks up his small suitcase and we all crowd the doorway, rushing to get out. Down the hallway again, past the sad people again, and out the door into the startling light of day.

"Do you mind if I drive, Dad?"

"No, honey, you go right ahead."

Franny takes the wheel of the car and off we go, back up the valley along the winding edges of first Wood and then Kalamalka Lake until we turn, finally, onto nineteenth street and pull up into our driveway. Mom is waiting, standing at the window.

April, 1974

John is standing in front of me listening to the band. I touch the elbow of his wool jacket, and for once not shy, ask, "Aren't you hot?"

"Yeah, I am a bit. Do you want to go for a walk?"

"Sure."

We leave the dance, walk down the steep hill to Kootenay Park and find a bench at the edge of the lake. The lake is dark and still. Elephant Mountain fills the sky. We sit side by side all night long, talking and listening.

It is the closest my face has ever been to John's.

In the early morning light, we walk back up the hill to the university. His hand cups my head and brushes the length of my hair, once, as we say good night.

Good Morning.

May, 1974

I go home to Vernon in May for the summer, to treeplant and save money. I think about John all the time and manage a short trip over to Nelson in July to see him. His wife has moved out from Toronto and they are going to try and live together again, to be together again, so I try and decide if I can go back to Nelson. According to my mother, I am preoccupied and moody all summer. She has no idea that in the last two weeks of term, I'd fallen in love with that *neat* English teacher I had written about in my letters home. In the end, I decide to go back. I like the art program and Nelson and it will be all right with John and me. I think I'll be able to handle it and get over him. After all, I'm only nineteen and he's married.

The night I arrive back in Nelson, I walk down the stairs of the Students' Union Building and into the dimly-lit pub. John's the first person I see, sitting with a group of people I know. He's sitting at the other end of the table, too far away from me to talk to. It isn't until we are all leaving that he comes over and asks if he can walk me home. When we are finally alone, he tells me his wife has moved back to Toronto and he is in Nelson by himself.

Each day is magical. We spend every minute we can together — our love is radiant; it seems to bathe everything and everyone around us in its glow.

It is listening to someone else's heart. Someone else's soul. Hearing the sound of it and wanting to hear it always. And finding out that that person, too, is listening to mine.

My second-year studio art courses are more demanding and require more time and effort. I'm enjoying them all and managing to get the assignments in on time, but their importance is secondary to the time John and I spend together. When John's not teaching and I'm not in class, we head out in the car, driving up and down the valley through the mountains. We meet in cafes during the day or bars at night, and on the weekends go hear live music in a club called The Mine Shaft. Inevitably, after whatever it is we've been doing, we end up at his small, rented house on Kootenay Lake, in bed.

May, 1975

In May, after our second year at NDU, John goes to the coast for the summer to use the UBC library for his research. I stay in Nelson to work and we see each other twice — once in Vancouver and once in Nelson. In the fall, John will be returning to Toronto to continue to work on his dissertation at York University and I've been accepted into the Fine Arts program at the University of Victoria. It will be all right. We know we'll be together again, sometime soon.

~~~~

I pack my bags, fly to Victoria, register at the university, and spend my first evening at the SUB pub with a friend from Vernon. I hate being there. It isn't Nelson. I don't like the program. I don't feel at home. John isn't there. I call him when I get back to the house.

"It's just awful."

"Well, you know, there's an Art School here in Toronto called 'Three Schools'. Artists run it. Why don't you think really carefully about it? You could come here, you know. You think about it and call me back."

I have decided before I hang up the phone.

I fly home unannounced, taking with me all the luggage I had carefully packed just the week before in Vernon for my year in Victoria. I am sound asleep in my old room when my parents return home and discover me. I've hidden my luggage in the closet so I don't have to face the music right away.

I say breezily to Mom, "Just thought I'd pop home and spend a couple more days with you and Dad before classes start."

That gets me a funny look.

Later in the evening, at the cabin, Mom and I are wrapped in blankets sitting outside on lawn chairs waiting for the moon to come up over the far hill. I tell her confidently, "This is what I want to do. This is what I am going to do."

Mom's expression changes to alarm. She says, "I can't say I think this is a good idea, Jude. He's still married. We haven't even met him. I don't want you to be hurt. You're going to have to tell your father."

I find Dad inside the cabin reading. I tell him my plans. He listens to the whole story without saying a word and then, "Honey, we've raised you kids to make your own decisions. And that means we have to have faith in your choices. You go to Toronto and be with John."

I had thought Mom was going to be the "cool" one and Dad was going to "freak out".

I chatter on about how much they're going to *love* him, how *wonderful* John is. By the time I get on the plane to fly to Toronto, they're *glad* to see me go. I just want to get there and apparently I haven't stopped letting them know this for the two long weeks I've been waiting to leave.

What neither of my parents tell me, even though they both know this is the one thing that'll keep me from going, is that Dad is in the first stages of a depression.

I've been too immersed in my own happiness to notice the signs.

September, 1975

We're sharing a flat on Shaftesbury Avenue with a young American exile. He had joined the United States Army on his own recognizance but quickly came to view his country's involvement in the Vietnam War as immoral. He defected to Canada, and in the eyes and policy of the American Army was branded a "deserter". He had, along with others who had found themselves in the same position, established Amex Canada in Toronto while continuing to work on his doctoral thesis in History. He tells me stories of other "deserters" and "dodgers", their desperate escapes to Canada in the middle of the night. He says I should be aware our phone is bugged. He also tells me that on occasion people will arrive at our door in the middle of the night, but that I shouldn't worry. He has learned to recognize a "criminal on the lam" from a person in need of legitimate help.

We are living in a "safe" house.

It doesn't take much to convince John to drag a heavy trunk in front of our bedroom door each night.

~~~~

We fix up a small room for John to write in. I tack an Indian cotton spread above the window for a curtain and drape my grandmother's hand-knitted wool blanket over an old couch. In another small room, we piece together a work desk (two sawhorses supporting an old door) for my painting and weaving projects.

John works every day on his dissertation, researching and writing it. I have never before seen someone concentrate with such focus or diligence. I've never known anyone so intrigued by something to want to do that.

During the week I ride the subway to my art classes and in the evenings we go to nightclubs and hear Jesse Winchester, or to concerts: Tom Waits, Bonnie Raitt, Bob Dylan and The Rolling Thunder Revue. Sometimes we go to the art school for night lectures where for the first time I hear contemporary artists talk about their work.

We attend the Miss General Idea Pageant extravaganza at the Art Gallery of Ontario and listen to the band, Rough Trade, sing "rough" songs. On the weekends, we go to The Lothian Muse for coffee or to Kensington Market for fruit and cheese or to "the island" with the rest of Toronto, or we walk a block from our flat, down into David Balfour Park and along trails knee-deep in brilliant red and yellow leaves.

Sometimes we make love all night long and in the morning when we first open our eyes and in the afternoon, too. I am swimming "golden" in love, in desire.

November, 1975

Walking in a park close to our house one day, I pause and sit down on the slope of a hill. I remove my mitts, place my hands on my knees, splay and flex the fingers. The finger which first went white in the cold when I was seventeen is red and swollen at the knuckles and so are all the others. They hurt when I bend or touch them. I wait. *There now.* I watch as each finger slowly turns white from tip to second knuckle, numb with cold. I put my mitts back on, rub my hands together and stuff them into my duffel coat pockets. Standing again, I jump up and down a few times to get the circulation going in my feet and pull my toque farther down over my ears. Tilting my face to the warmth of the sun, I wonder *how can I be this cold, dressed in all these layers of winter clothing?*

When I return home, I go upstairs to our bedroom and sit on the bed. I take my arms out of my T-shirt sleeves, cross them over my breasts and place my hands under my armpits. Soon, my fingers begin to throb. After a few minutes, I withdraw my hands and study the fingers, reddish purple and burning now. *They're on fire.* My eyes water. In a few minutes the pain begins to ebb as my skin gradually returns to its normal colour. As if nothing had happened.

I grab two sweaters and pull them on as I leave the room and walk into my small studio. Picking up several different-coloured balls of wool, I hold them against each other until I find a combination I like, then pick up a ball of strong hemp and begin lacing it over the small nails of my loom frame.

December, 1975

"Is Dad feeling all right?"

"No, honey. He's in a depression. He has been since early fall."

"But you didn't tell me."

"No."

A few minutes later, I hang up the phone and turn to John. "I have to go home. My dad's sick."

~~~~

I'm leaning over the front seat of the car between my father, who's driving, and my mother in the passenger seat. It's the middle of the night and my parents have just picked me up at the bus depot in Salmon Arm where I'd been bused from Calgary. The plane hadn't been able to land at the Kelowna airport because of dense fog and had flown back to Calgary.

Salmon Arm, about ninety miles north of Vernon, was the closest town the bus driver would take me to. He was in a bad mood. He'd been summoned from his home at midnight to drive this unfamiliar route through heavy snow.

I'm chattering non-stop about my life in Toronto with John. Dad's grunting an occasional "huh"! keeping his eyes on the road and Mom is fully engaged, asking questions, exclaiming, and laughing.

As I write the previous two lines, a familiar voice inside me speaks up. *But didn't you come home because your father was ill?*

Yes.

Then why aren't you asking them about that?

Because Dad's depressions, when they occurred, were always just "there". We all just carried on. It doesn't mean that I was unaware or uncaring.

Are you sure about that?

Okay. I admit after a few days at home, I just wanted to be back in Toronto with John. Defensively, *But there was nothing I could do for Dad. His depressions had to run their course.*

Well, what about your mother?

With surprise, *Mom was fine. She was always fine.*

Are you sure about that?

At the time, I was.

What happened next?

Franny and Len and Joe arrived home from wherever they were living and we all had Christmas together.

What was that like?

It was the same as it always was except Dad was quieter than usual and would sleep a lot in the middle of the day.

What happened after Christmas?

Franny and Joe and Len left and then it was just me and my parents.

How were you feeling? I mean physically.

Impatiently, *My joints hurt and sometimes I felt very tired for no reason. You already know that.*

Didn't that worry you?

I thought I was just pining for John. Okay?

Okay. I just wanted to clarify the situation.

January 1976

I drive down the valley, meet John at the airport and we head back up to Vernon, bringing each other up to date on what has happened in our lives since we last talked, which would have been on the phone the night before. John had decided he could use a break from his thesis after Christmas and now we have two whole weeks together.

We walk over the Commonage, snow crunching beneath our feet, and find the pond where I used to skate as a child. We tap our boots on its edge until the thin ice cracks and breaks; pieces of it float in the dark water. John picks up a branch and swishes it around, makes a motion to splash me. I throw snow at him. We hear a sudden flap of wings, a duck lifts from the reeds across the pond and quacks our presence through the air.

This is so right.

A few days later, we take the bus to Vancouver to join my parents. They're staying in a friend's house for a month while she's away on a trip. Mom is hoping the change in environment will lift Dad's spirits.

John will be meeting my parents for the first time.

~~~~

I whisper, "Don't drink too much tonight, okay?"

John flashes his cocky grin and says, "I won't if you don't."

"Ha-Ha. Very funny. Here we are!"

"So soon?" John gives me a look of exaggerated terror.

I jump out of the cab, "Come on. They're going to love you."

I know everything's going to be fine when Mom reaches out to shake John's hand, changes her mind, and kisses him on the cheek. My father steps forward, formally shakes John's hand and says, without a trace of sarcasm in his voice, "It's good to finally meet you, Son."

~~~~

A doctor in Vernon had made an appointment for me to see an immunologist while we're in Vancouver. I'm sitting on the examining table in a white hospital gown. Dr. Patrick gently bends my arm and leg joints while querying me about the poor circulation in my fingers and the soreness in my finger joints. I've been experiencing pain in my knee joints for a few weeks now, too.

He leaves the room while I dress, returns a few minutes later and sits down across from me.

"What's happening in your life right now?"

"I'm living in Vernon for a few months until my boyfriend drives out from Ontario in June. We're going back to Toronto for the summer and then we're not sure where we'll be after that."

"You have arthritis of some kind. It's looking like rheumatoid arthritis but I need to have more information before making a diagnosis. It is *imperative* that you keep in close contact with a doctor wherever you're living."

~~~~

While we're in Vancouver, Mom tells me a doctor there has put Dad on a new drug called lithium. Apparently, it has been quite successful in levelling out the highs and lows of manic depression. Dad will know the medication is working if the depression lifts and he doesn't go into the manic stage in the spring.

As for my own news, we all go into a kind of frozen denial. We don't discuss it too much because we still don't know exactly what we're dealing with and I imagine we're all just hoping my problems will somehow just disappear. But there is worry in Mom and Dad's eyes and John has become remarkably close to them during this short time together.

~~~~

My parents drop us off at the Greyhound bus station in Vancouver, and sixteen hours later we arrive in Nelson for a visit with our good friends, Kayda and Peter.

We're staying in a motel across Kootenay Lake and close to the orange bridge. Late one morning, we're lying in bed watching TV. Someone is being elected leader of the Tory party. His head fills the screen and when he speaks it's in a self-effacing, almost shy manner. He's excited though, hopeful-looking. His name is Joe Clark.

The aching begins in my shoulders, reaches down my arm muscles and into my wrists. John warms oil on the stove, dips his fingers into it, smoothes it over my skin.

July, 1976

In old houses all along Brunswick Avenue, people like us are covering their things, packing towels and sheets into boxes, emptying cupboards, moving out for three days while the exterminators deal with the annual cockroach infestation.

We walk through the sticky heat, down Bloor, to the Royal Ontario Museum, to the sanctuary of its cool, clean exhibition rooms.

I have a cold that lasts all summer. It turns into something called atypical pneumonia. But this exhaustion is something else. I can't understand it. I can't even describe it. Two summers ago I had been tree planting, hiking up and down a mountain in the Shuswap all day long, carrying a big bag of seedlings and a shovel. I had been tanned and strong, the most physically fit I had ever been. My dad was so proud of his tree-planting daughter; he was always after my sister and I, "Play a sport. Get those muscles working!"

~~~~

Mid-August, John receives a call from the University of Regina, offering him a Sessional, teaching literature. He accepts. A few days later, a letter arrives for me from the university, which tells me I've been accepted into the third year of their BFA program. I'd also sent away for some information on an American-run art school on a small island in Greece.

I choose Regina.

Late August, 1976

John and I drive back out west to Edmonton and then Vernon, collect our things and return to Regina where we find a small house to rent. One minute I'm fine, having fun — we leave the city, head out onto the prairie to check out the new landscape, or go and explore the university — and the next, my body just drains of all energy, goes weak. Weaker than weak. Like my spine is a pin trying to hold me up. I feel sick to my stomach.

When the fall semester starts, I leave a drawing class one morning, vomit in the washroom and return to class. Later, I find John in his office and he drives me to our rented house. I don't understand any of it and I can see the uncertainty in John's eyes, too.

After waking suddenly — twice in one week — in the middle of the night, nauseous, barely reaching the bathroom before throwing up, I make an appointment with a GP, recommended by the Women's Centre at the university.

~~~~

I'm sitting in her office and she's chomping on peanuts (the odour permeates the room). She's telling me, "I can't just send you to a rheumatologist. How will I look if you don't have rheumatoid arthritis? I have my reputation to think of. Your hands don't look arthritic."

I say nervously, "But my joints hurt all the time and I'm throwing up for no reason."

She smiles in a way that I find irritating, "Are you homesick?"

"No!" *I'm in love you idiot.*

"I'm going to give you a prescription for Valium, twenty 2 mg pills, and no, I don't do routine pap tests until you're thirty."

She doesn't order any tests of any kind.

Tears are streaming down my face all the way home on the bus, and I'm thinking, *Well, it's official now. I'm nuts.*

When I reach our house, John isn't home yet and I stand in the middle of the kitchen with the red linoleum floor, and slowly turn round and round, stomach constricting, heart emptying.

~~~~

We call Dr. Patrick in Vancouver and he says to contact CARRS. They will refer me to a rheumatologist. And to find another GP immediately.

I am referred to Dr. McMann at the Rheumatology Clinic in Regina. In the waiting room, I see a lot of older people with gnarled hands. Dr. McMann asks me reams of questions which seem unconnected. He says something about a "butterfly rash" on my face. I have no idea what he's talking about. He doesn't explain and I don't ask him to. *Is that sympathy I see in his eyes? Why sympathy?* I give him what I think is a neutral, everything's OK kind of smile, and go to the lab holding a requisition for blood tests in my hand. After several vials of my blood are taken, John and I go home, none the wiser.

End of fall term, 1976

We're sitting in his office looking at my drawings spread out on the floor around us. Walter Stahl, my instructor, is saying, "You're okay, pretty good, but you're probably never going to set the world on fire." A small smile accompanies a small wink.

Little does he know, nor I for that matter, that the world already is on fire. It's been set for me. There's a Wolf running ahead of the flames through the dry prairie grass. He's ravenous. He's almost upon me. Even now he's reaching out a hooked claw, and with feral precision, splicing my skin, clamping his jaw on bone joint. Igniting red pain. Arthritis. I am twenty, my soul and body unprepared for the wildfire to come. My bones are kindling; it's just a matter of time, it's only going to take a small shift in the wind for the wildfire to catch up to and engulf me.

Later that night, hurt, I tell John about Stahl's critique.

He asks, "Walter who?"

"Walter Stahl."

"Walter who?"

"You know. My drawing instructor. The one who . . . oh."

We exchange a look.

John says, "Exactly."

December, 1976

A few days before we're to go to Vernon for Christmas, we receive a bill from Dr. McMann's clinic. We are out of province; otherwise the bill would never have been mailed directly to us. There is a fee and typed beneath that: *suspected Systemic Lupus Erythematosus.* My heart stops. John's face pales and then he becomes furious, "God Damn it, they send a possible diagnosis on a God Damn bill!" *Systemic Lupus Erythematosus.* Those three words are like gunshots blasting into our lives. We have never heard them before and they sound terrifying.

Wolf is closing in.

John calls the clinic and speaks to Dr. McMann's nurse. She is mortified, flustered. The doctor can't see me in the next couple of days, but as soon as we get back from our holiday we should come right in. We stuff it all inside and head for my parents in Vernon. Mom says later, that when she first saw me, she was alarmed — she'd seen me just four months ago and I'm even thinner now. My joints are aching. I'm pale and tense. And cold. I'm always so cold.

My father is a pharmacist and he has a Merck Manual in the house. But Dad's been retired for almost six years and the book is outdated, had been published in the '50s. The four of us are sitting in the living room, passing it around. Everyone is being very quiet. Not saying a word, not looking at each other. I'm sitting on the floor in front of the fireplace poking the flaming logs around with the iron poker. When John passes the Manual to me and I begin to read, I don't understand most of the medical terminology, but I do understand the words which say roughly, *Until recently, lupus patients could expect a prognosis of five years but now, there is data to show most patients are still living, unless they have kidney or central nervous system involvement, ten years after diagnosis.* Then the words blur and look like small black bugs jerking their way across the page. A glowing ember spits from the fire onto my jean leg. I flick it off and smash it out with the poker.

Most patients. Not all. But I haven't been diagnosed. There is still that.

Valentine's Day, 1977

I am at the university all day making clay bowls. My finger joints hurt more than usual as I prepare the wet clay, knead, and whack hunks of it against the tabletop, listen for the sound of the last air bubble popping. I form equal-sized spheres in my hands, carry one over to the potter's wheel, settle myself on the seat and start the wheel turning with a foot-kick. Tiny bits of grit burn the edges of my hands as I press the clay, centring it on the steel disc. Soon, both arms begin to ache from wrists to shoulder blades. I continue making bowls until I've completed the assignment, then pack up quickly and leave for home.

Later in the evening, the pain sharpens, and spreads into my chest. We try to distract ourselves — begin watching the movie, *Love Story,* from our foamy on the floor, but halfway through, John turns it off. We've seen it before. We know how it ends. The pain is unbearable, like a knife twisting inside my heart with every breath I take. It's worse when I lie down. John sits up with me all night, stroking my back.

In the morning, we drive straight to Dr. McMann, at the clinic. He listens to my heart and after x-rays are taken, sends us to the hospital. Diagnosis: pericarditis — inflammation of the lining surrounding the heart. I'm given 100 mg of an anti-inflammatory drug called prednisone, and two hours later, the pain is completely gone. Every small breath feels sweet and pure and painless. I finally sleep.

Over the next two days, my doctor asks me more questions and orders more tests. Then finally, the results are conclusive.

Wolf is upon me. The wildfire is burning all around and through me.

But with this terrible knowledge comes a strange kind of solace. It is official. I am not nuts. Every odd physical occurrence over the last four years can be explained. Can be validated.

~~~~

It is not the good tiredness after a game of tennis. The invigorating tiredness of a morning spent digging in the garden. Or even the satisfying tiredness of swimming thirty-six pool laps.

This tiredness is in a class all of its own.

Every cell feels like it's coated with some thick matter, making my blood heavy and sluggish, a weight.

It's like there's a thin grey mesh throughout my body and the blood has to push its way through this mesh to give me the energy just to move. Every cell is exhausted with the effort.

It is the tiredness of a body at odds with an element, a body trying to swim upstream against the current.

At the beginning, in my twenties, I wake up in the morning feeling this way. I carry this fatigue through every part of every day, soldier on smiling, and inside, feel more and more distanced from everything and everybody around me. To anyone looking in on one of my painting classes, I would appear to be just another student, laughing along with the others at some crazy joke. And when I'm standing alone at my canvas, brushing great gobs of paint over its surface, I am focused, oblivious to everything else going on around me, until some sudden wave of nausea or abrupt depletion of energy claims my attention. Glancing over at the other art students and seeing their energy, the energy I used to have, I feel separate. Different. *This disease is not going to go away. I will never feel like myself again.*

I will have to work twice as hard to be the person I want to be. Thus begins the charade. I'm honest with John — most of the time — but to the rest of the world I present a different front. I'm not even honest with my doctors. I rarely talk about the physical pain I'm in. I can hide (or think I can) this fatigue from people. Rise to the occasion. And inside, be desperate to just lay my head down, to allay a profound weariness. I think, *If I can just go to sleep, and sleep for days or months, however long it takes, my body might recover and I could wake up well.*

(Today, more than twenty years later, I still have this fantasy.)

But because I'm young and afraid and tense and judging myself, I cannot relax. I try to rest in the afternoons, but as soon as I lie down my mind begins turning over a hundred morbid thoughts. I'm often more tired when I get up than when I lie down. At least when I'm up, I'm distracted, doing things. When I lie down, it's just me and my brain.

I have no appetite and although I've always been thin, I look now like the original Little Match Girl, a pale waif with long brown hair. There is a photograph of me holding Alice, John's Kerry-blue Terrier, in the kitchen of our rented flat in Regina. I look at that young woman and know two things: she is in love with the young man taking the picture, and every day she is feeling a little more lost, more afraid of what is waiting there, in the shadows, for him and her.

~~~~

I have a night class and I'm standing at the bus stop, huddled in my borrowed red parka. John is teaching at the main campus. It's the middle of winter. Prairie wind. Prairie cold. A plastic bag skitters down the empty road past me. I imagine a movie: It's 1886, a small homestead on the prairies. John and I are the struggling young pioneers; we've built the log house, we've run out of food and John (of course, the man has to go) has inched his way, tied to a rope, out into the raging prairie snowstorm to get the last bag of potatoes from the barn. We had seen a movie just like it the summer before we moved to Regina! My joints are pulsing with pain and I think, *Maybe this isn't the best climate in the world for me. Regina, mid-winter. Where is my beautiful warm Okanagan Valley?*

~~~~

I call it Gypsy arthritis. It never stays in one place long. First, only my fingers are affected and I develop large, blue, watery swells of inflammation on the backs of my hands. Then my wrist, elbow, knee and ankle joints are attacked.

Wolf is uncommonly skillful — he selects corresponding joints on each side of my body and clamps down hard, simultaneously, on the exact same spot on each. Is this a two-headed Wolf?

I have to go up and down stairs all day in the Fine Arts Building. On the bad days, each step has to be maneuvered so as to put the least amount of weight on whichever joint or joints is involved. If I pass someone on the stairwell and we accidentally bump elbows, I wince, hold my breath until the pain subsides.

The inflammation usually lasts two or three days in one or two joints and then moves on to a different area. I lightly press the sore spots, trying to massage the pulsing, sharp pain to a duller ache. My friend, Rhonda, remembers me continually kneading my wrists and fingers. She remembers my thinness, and the way I always shivered in the cold. Every Sunday morning, she or Ian would phone, wanting to meet us at the Quality Tearoom for breakfast. John would leap out of bed, dress quickly, and go ahead to join them. A while later, I'd drag myself out of bed, dress, and head out the front door.

Now, twenty-four years later, Rhonda says, "It's so clear in my head, I could paint a picture. We could see your front door from the café. Eventually, you would appear and begin walking over the frozen, empty Safeway parking lot. You'd have your red parka on. I couldn't see your face because of the hood and the thick ruff of fur surrounding it. Your long hair was the only thing recognizably 'you', hanging loose down the front of your coat."

I would say I had significant arthritis for about ten years, between 1975 and 1986. Often, over those years, I couldn't walk a few blocks because of the pain in my knee or ankle joints. I couldn't play tennis, which I loved, or even consider cross-country skiing which our friends were beginning to take up.

After 1986, the arthritis left my body just as mysteriously as it had first appeared. It hadn't deformed my bones. *Wolf can be forgiving.* Did the arthritis burn itself out? Did my maintenance dosages of steroids and immunosuppressives keep it under control? Was it just the nature of the disease? So few answers.

August, 1977

It's the last day of university break. John and I have been staying at the cabin on the lake. We've had two idyllic months — lazy days, alternately baking in the sun on the pier and diving into the clear, aqua water to cool off. It seems as if every last bit of inflammation in my joints has been soothed away by the healing touch of the sun's rays. My hair is sun-streaked, my skin tanned brown and I feel rested, healthy.

But today we have to leave, have to return to Regina for another university year. We've packed up and are standing on the lawn looking out at the lake — I'm loath to leave this summer paradise for another prairie winter, where the arthritis will surely return. I'm thinking of that icy drive we take from our rented flat to the university every morning when the car jerks along as if on square wheels, the hairs in my nostrils freeze and the tips of my fingers turn white inside my mitts.

"Let's do it."

"Are you serious?"

"Yes. Come on! Let's go!"

I drop my clothes in a heap on the grass and run naked across the sand into the water. John looks around furtively and does the same. We're laughing and splashing each other. The lake is a deep bowl of shifting blues and greens. Diamonds are sparkling off the surface, in the midday sun. Minnows are dancing in the darkness below us. Fingertips touch, bodies wrap, and we turn in the delicious wetness of it.

~~~~

How could I know that this was to be my last "free" summer in the sun before I developed the severe photosensitivity that can be a manifestation of lupus. The next summer, back again in the Okanagan and staying at the lake, I burn for the first time. I'm caught off-guard. I've always tanned to a deep brown. I don't recognize this sick feeling, my cheeks fiery red and blistering by nightfall. Sun exposure can cause a flare. I think the sun has been responsible for two of the four flares that have affected my kidney function. Both have occurred at the end of a long, hot summer, and perhaps because I hadn't been careful enough.

I learn to avoid the sun with sunscreen, hats, early morning walks, and evening swims. Now, at the beginning of the 21st century, everyone, if not afraid, is aware of the danger of ultraviolet rays, and I have lots of company in the shade under trees. But at the beginning, in my twenties, it was just another thing that made me feel isolated and alone.

I grew up in a pastoral landscape of orchards, brilliant suns, and cool, blue-green lakes. I, too, was that child in Dylan Thomas's "Fern Hill". We spent every summer, from the day after school got out in June until the day before Labour Day, at the cabin on the lake. We *lived* in the sun.

Labour Day, "Grey Ditch", 1958 (age 3)

The sun, high in the blue sky, beams down on me. It tickles and warms my face, burnishing my skin golden brown. A grasshopper lands on a blade of tall yellow grass beside me. The air is humming with bugs and pungent with the musky smells of late summer. I'm sitting beside the dry ditch, picking a burr out of my white sock, and every time I tug at the burr, my sock stretches out and then thwacks back against my leg. Dust puffs into the air. I'm mesmerized.

Len is sitting beside me scratching our dog and laughing as Binky's jaw snaps uselessly in the air, trying to catch a late summer fly circling lazily in the air above her nose.

Nearby, Cee-Cee is dreamily poking a stick around in the dirt and every now and then she picks up a green or rust-coloured stone and places it in a pile with some others.

We hear a whoop, "I got another one!" and Jo-Jo races back from farther down, from the shady spot where he's been sitting perfectly still for an eternity, waiting for his prey. He dangles a greeny-brown salamander in my face as he rushes by.

I look over to Mom and Dad. They're sitting cross-legged on the ground drinking Ginger Ale from bottles. They both grin as Jo-Jo rushes up with his catch. I crunch a few salty potato chips in my mouth from the bag beside me, take a sip of my Orange Crush, and skip over to join them.

~~~~

Now I plan every activity of every day to avoid the sun all year round. In the spring, before the leaves have burst, it always seems impossible to me. If I'm caught in the sun, I feel like I'm standing in or walking through poison, that the heat and light coating my skin and penetrating my body is a lethal substance, triggering my immune system to react wrongly — against itself.

Every summer, every year, since 1977

Nieces and nephews and friends' kids are yelling and splashing around in the lake. My brother, Joe, has taken a lounge chair out and is lying on it, baking in the sun, at the end of the pier. Adults and kids are continually going in and out of the cabin to get cold drinks, in and out of the water to cool off.

I'm sitting swaddled in protective clothing beneath the willow tree. And I'm pissed off.

Midday, I stride out to join Joe at the end of the pier. I lie down on my back and lift my face to the sun. For a minute or two, I fight fire with fire. Reduce the dangerous, red sphere high in the sky to a harmless white cinder. See it float away. Gone. Forever. But I couldn't live without light. Nothing can live without light.

My sister, Franny, always notices. "Jude?" She calls to me . . . "Jude."

"I know. It's just for a second. I'll be right in," I answer.

~~~~

For years I continue to go to the lake midday. I wear light, protective clothing. Even in the shade, I slather myself with sunscreen. I pull a straw hat down low over my face. I sit in the deepest shade of the willow tree with my back to the glare off the water and an umbrella tipped overhead. And still my skin itches.

My skin itches when I'm downtown and have to leave my car to walk across an exposed parking lot.

Sixty seconds in the sun and Wolf is there, licking my face with small flames.

Now I go to the lake after four or five o'clock in the evening when the sun begins to drop behind the hills. I can swim then.

September, 1978

Thinking she can still escape the flames, the wolf changes direction. Instinctively, she heads west, towards the mountains. Here now. A forest. She enters, crashes deeper and deeper into its heart, thinking its darkness will save her. Stopping to catch her breath, she hears only the sound of her own heart beating crazily against her chest.

By the end of our second year living in Regina, I am exhausted from trying to keep up with the demands of three studio art classes and two academic courses. I'm exhausted from the effort of living day to day with the unpredictable physical symptoms of lupus while trying to give the impression there isn't anything wrong with me.

I want to leave the prairie winters behind and go home to the Okanagan where my family is. I just want to be near them until John and I can get a handle on this disease. I wonder now how I thought we were going to be able to do that. Did I still harbour hope that this disease could be made to go away? Or that it was all just a bad dream? Or even just a really bad mistake? At the time, we think we'll stay a year, then head out for some other place, some other adventure.

John mails his c.v. to the community college in Vernon and is offered one course teaching literature. We stay with my parents for a couple of weeks until the flat we've rented is available. One morning, I wake with a familiar feeling in my chest. It isn't quite as bad as the pericarditis pain I'd experienced two years ago, but it feels like it's in the same place. The doctor, an old friend of my parents, makes a *house* call! After examining me, he arranges to have me admitted to hospital for tests: diagnosis — pleurisy. He orders more tests, blood and urine. A nurse asks me if my urine is always that dark. My heart quickens. *Wolf is near.* The doctor tells me I am showing signs of kidney disease and he'd like to send me to Vancouver to see a nephrologist. He has already made an appointment for next week with a Dr. Ballard. My heart beats faster and the nurse comes in and sits with me until John comes.

Is this it? Is this how Wolf will finally do me in? I am undefended.

John arrives and the vulnerability about his mouth and eyes makes me cry.

Before we leave for Vancouver, Franny's husband, Don, calls and says he wants to take us out for dinner. When we arrive at the restaurant, there is a huge bouquet of flowers sitting in the middle of our table. Don had arranged for them and also for the waitress to bring us a bottle of champagne in a bucket of ice. For two hours, the four of us laugh as we always have, and for an entire evening I don't think of the future. This is Don's biggest gift to John and I.

We go to Vancouver. A kidney biopsy reveals chronic, progressive kidney disease, a manifestation of lupus. Massive dosages of steroids are prescribed. It takes twelve months to overcome Wolf. Finally, he is chemicalled out of my body and the inflammation is stopped. There has been some loss of kidney function. Nothing to worry about yet. *Yet.* This does nothing to console me. I visualize an egg timer. The sand is almost all at the top but the grains are slowly sifting down. *How long will it take? Will I need dialysis? Are kidney transplants possible with lupus patients? Will I die?* The familiar red neon in my brain, flashing its questions and fears. I am twenty-three years old.

~~~~

I tap out the phone number of the pharmacy and when my brother Len answers, I say, "Hi there. It's me. I need some refills on my prescriptions."

"Okay, I'll just get your file. How are you feeling?"

"All right."

Christmas, 1973

In the morning, I open Len's present to me and discover a dictionary. He says dryly, "I just thought since you're a 'university girl' now, you're going to be hearing all those big university words and you'll want to know what they mean."

Later in the day, I'm sprawled on the living room floor, rifling through a box of chocolates, trying to guess which ones are the creams. Len's slouched in an armchair nearby and we're playing our new game.

All I have to say to start us off is, "Well, at university . . . "

And Len says, "antihistamine!"

I give him, "stream-of-consciousness!"

Len states, "That's not a word. It's a phrase." But from the look on his face, I don't think he knows what it means. Aha! One for me.

Alternating turns, we draw each syllable of each word out, sounding as snobbish, as brilliantly intelligent as we can.

"Well then, how about, epiphany?"

"anticoagulant!"

"microcosm!"

"tetracycline!"

I'm running out of big words, "gymnasium!"

"Yeah, right, Jude. Nice try."

~~~~

Once a week I fill a red plastic pillbox with my medications. The box has seven vertical compartments, one for
each day of the week, and each has a sliding clear plastic
top. There are four slots in each compartment for
different times of the day. I count out the pills, the correct
dosages for each medication, and drop them into their
correct time slots. The multicoloured pills form a
repeated grid pattern across the box.

These are the medication dosages I take daily when
I'm in remission. Then there are the ones I take when the
lupus is active, my kidneys flaring. Then, I take higher
doses of just about everything. There are several different
pills for hypertension, pills for water retention, pills to
help me sleep (they don't work), pills to stop my tremor
(they don't work), calcium for my bones (to replace what
the steroids take away), and Vitamin D, as well as pills to
suppress the kidney inflammation and pills to suppress
my immune system. Steroids and Immunosuppressives.
For life. For life. A blessing and a sentence. I swallow a
handful of pills first thing in the morning, a smaller
handful at suppertime and another, smaller handful at
bedtime.

I take eight times the amount of my usual maintenance dosage of prednisone when a flare involves my
kidneys. Prednisone is my miracle drug, the one that
prevents me from going into complete kidney failure.
Without it, I would have reached end-stage renal failure
years ago. It is also the drug that causes more visible harm
and more inner turmoil than the kidney disease itself.
Paradox. I think it ironic that the subsequent physical,

mental, and emotional chaos I experience comes from these little round white pills, from this orderly and innocuously patterned pillbox.

It's like the box and its contents are a formal, geometric Vasarely painting and once the pills are swallowed and dissolved in my system, they transform my brain into a Jackson Pollock, a jumble of electric energy, an expressionist "splatter".

Within a few days, the speediness begins. My body and mind are winding up. I experience a kind of euphoria at first. My mind is jumping. Chattering to John, full of ideas, "You know John, I think I'm *smarter* on prednisone!" Big laughs and grins which save the day, but this is not fun and I can't imagine what it's like for him. I can't sleep — three hours at a time at the most. I'm up most of the night sitting in the dark. In the morning, I can't hold my coffee cup; my whole body is shaking. I don't stop drinking coffee, won't give up this small pleasure. My muscles weaken and dark bruises appear spontaneously on my legs. At the beginning, my racing metabolism causes me to lose ten pounds.

Then, the prednisone increases my appetite; I'm ravenous. I eat and eat. *I* am *Wolf.*

I regain the ten pounds I initially lost, and over the next six months gain twenty-five more. I am devastated by the way I look. None of my clothes fit. I find an old pair of sweats and wear John's old shirts. I try to hide my body. My face is a swollen moon called Cushing's Syndrome, a side effect of high doses of prednisone. It's like there's a tiny pump under the skin of my face. Each day a little more pressure is applied. My skin stretches and bloats.

Soon, I can no longer recognize myself in the mirror and I imagine that one day my face will become a full, featureless, empty moon, and I will, quite simply, disappear.

People don't always recognize me on the street. One day, I run into an acquaintance of my mother's, who announces gleefully, "Jude, you've gotten stout!"

I tell myself, *Come on, come on, you can get through this. The drugs have made you well. Hang on, hang on. This too, shall pass.*

I don't know who I am anymore.

~~~~

August — Lupus flaring. Kidneys failing. Could this be a short "blip" flare, or the usual year from beginning to full recovery? Swallow the pills. Believe they'll work, don't think about the shaking, the weight loss, the weight gain, the sleepless nights, the nightmare dreams. Try not to look in the mirror. Moonface. Fatface. Becoming unrecognizable to others but most of all to myself. Bruised legs. The crinkle of stretch marks across either hip. Pot belly. Swollen breasts. Naked, I think I look pregnant but there is no baby growing inside me. Zits on my face and rash on my chest. Mind speeding. Morbid thoughts, morbid images. This is crazy. I feel crazy. Crazy for sweets, crazy for any kind of food. Gaining weight day by day. This isn't my Wolf turning me ravenous. This is some other Wolf from some other pack making me never full, never satisfied. Every night for months, the bogeyman waking me with his dark presence — standing in the doorway, standing at the end of the bed — "John, he's there! This time there's really someone there." "No, Jude, it's just a dream, it's OK, it's just a dream." This dark presence with me during the day now, too, a slight shadow hanging over me, making me nervous, vaguely afraid. I can't do this. I can do this. September — Jitters building, hands trembling. Should stop drinking coffee. Don't stop drinking coffee. 3 a.m. Ping! Every morning, waking wide-eyed alert, moving from our bed to the living-room couch, curling up in the green cotton blanket. 4 a.m. Cleaning cupboards, sorting drawers, closets, bathroom cupboards, organizing studio, sometimes even ironing. 6:30 a.m. Grinding coffee. Filling the pot with water and the filter with coffee. Pressing the "on" button. Waking John. Sitting together and talking. This is golden-time when it's still dark outside and John's beside me and the world isn't moving too fast yet. December — Finally, the inflammation in my kidneys is stopped. After my blood work and urine tests indicate sustained good results for several months, my doctors tell me it's safe to begin reducing the prednisone. Slowly. They mean excruciatingly slowly. Each morning, hopeful, standing on the weigh scales. Six more weeks and maddeningly, the needle stays stuck on the same number — twenty-five pounds over my normal weight. Finally, over the next few weeks, I lose ten pounds. *Must be water.* Now I can't get enough sleep. I can't stay awake. I have the strange sensation that the only thing holding my eyes open is a couple of strategically placed toothpicks and if they were to be knocked out, my eyelids would snap shut. This is a fatigue like never before.

There's a Wolf snarling, "Baby, you thought you were tired before. Now catch this! And this!" The Wolf loads me up until I can't lift myself out of bed. This isn't my Wolf, either. This is yet another Wolf from yet another pack. I don't recognize his low growl, the heartless yellow eyes, the cold, hard claws snagging my body, dragging me behind him over the grey earth, through an airless landscape.

April — I venture out for my first walk in months. Halfway down the block, my muscles are screaming. I'm out of breath. My hip joints are stiff; my bones feel clunky. *I'm Tin Man. I need a few squirts of oil.* I return home, try it again the next morning, same thing. I skip a day, then walk a little farther the next. Each day a little farther. Finally, after a few weeks, my impatience overriding the pain, I decide to keep on walking. *I'm gonna walk beyond this pain.* A few blocks farther the pain begins to ebb. By the time I've circled the neighbourhood and opened our patio gate, I'm flushed with victory. A few weeks later, I'm loving these morning walks, feeling stronger, beginning to believe I can get well. *breathe the air trust the air the air can make you well take deep breaths dip into your spirit-well sprinkle your soul with cool clear water these are my childhood streets I'm walking so long ago the child in the photograph smiling composed confident hands clasped lightly smiling for daddy you would think nothing could be wrong in this child's world but no daddy is already getting sick the autumn descent the winter depression he's slowly pacing the hallway pacing the house hands wringing or clamped shut long afternoon sleeps when he goes away from us leaves us for what has to be a happier world why else would he go daddy please don't leave don't go asking mommy at bedtime is daddy dying mommy is daddy dying no darling daddy isn't dying he's melancholy that means he's a little bit sad darling he will get better he will get better go to sleep now hush now I'll hold your hand until you fall asleep later waking up alone in the dark hallway heart pounding it's always the same nightmare I'm crying paralyzed I can't get through the dark thinking dreaming I was dying I couldn't breathe caught in tangled ropes forever now its manic-spring daddy's moving fast now moving at the speed of light making up for lost time but still taking the time to hold me close and now its idyllic-summer two months of daddy peaceful, calm, recognizable again honeybunch I'll watch you swim the "log"' now let's see you go kick hard that's the way and later which "old man story" would you like me to tell you tonight until some other autumn and it all begins again . . .*

July — I'm swimming now. Out to the farthest yellow buoy. Two times there and back, between the buoy and the raft, a slow breaststroke, the quiet intake and release of my own breathing the only sound in my ears. The faintly punkish taste of lake-water in my mouth. Parallel to the pumphouse, I pass over the great, brown, algae-covered water pipes jutting from the shore and beneath me. The pipes cut underwater across my path and for a second, I shiver, have the same eerie feeling I had as a child swimming over these same pipes. *Something could be down there. It could just reach up and grab my ankle.* It would be so easy to alter or just shorten my route a little bit. But I never do. I *always* swim over the pipes. On the way back, flipping over, kicking hard, strong arms wheeling backwards through the silken water. I stop kicking and float for a few minutes, eyes open to the sky. *It's cyan tonight.* My body feels weightless and the calm inside me matches the calm around me. *There now. This is your element. Water.* Turning over and kicking again I reach the raft and grab my kickboard. Two more times to the last buoy and back, moving now as if being propelled by a small-powered engine through the water. Turning in towards shore, I see our nieces and nephews playing bocce on the lawn, our sheepdog, Georgia, rooting around in the sand by the water's edge and the adults watching the kids, drinking coffee and eating pie. Every now and then I hear a triumphant squeal followed by enthusiastic clapping as someone gains a point.

September — I'm there. In remission. *Wolf has retreated, the wildfire controlled.*

~~~~

Sometime during a flare in 1992, I begin to wonder about the high and low cycle that prednisone throws me into. The medication seems to set up a kind of pseudo manic depression pattern, very close to the one my father went through year after year. Lithium levelled out my father's chemical imbalance. Fortunately, my symptoms disappear when I'm finally off the high doses of prednisone. *Is this what manic depression feels like? Daddy, is this what it was like for you?* I want my father here with me tonight so I can tell him I think I understand now. So I can comfort him.

November, 1978

I'm a mess. My GP makes the necessary arrangements for me to see a psychiatrist in town. The first time I go to the doctor's office, I'm terrified I'm going to run into someone I know. Then they'll know I'm crazy. *I must be crazy — I'm in a psychiatrist's office.* I like the doctor, but my attitude is, the only way I'm going to feel better is if someone can remove this disease from my body. I know this doctor doesn't have the power to do that, so, really, what's the point? How can talking make anything better? After three sessions, I think, *Well, that's enough of that. I'll be all right now. On with my life.* I can still hear the put-on cheerfulness of my voice when the psychiatrist calls after two months to ask how I'm doing. "Oh, fine. Just great. Yes, I'm just fine."

I'm not just fine, but I think the best way to deal with this disease is to pretend, on the outside, that I don't have it. I rarely mention it to my closest friends. If I do, it's in a breezy way, as if it is nothing.

It is everything. It consumes my thoughts and directs my every action. I can't rid myself of its presence in these early years. The whole weight of it — the arthritis, the fatigue, the threat of kidney failure and the fact that I can't walk a few blocks in the sun without real danger — is pushing down on me, threatening to cripple the life I had imagined for John and I.

I torment myself. I find a hundred things to worry about. I know so little about the disease except that there's a lot to worry about. There is little information for patients at this time, and even if I hadn't been afraid to ask, my doctors couldn't have told me what path my disease would follow. They don't know. In fact, my doctors tell me not to read about it, which just increases my fear. *What are they not telling me?*

I spin a cocoon around John and myself. I feel safe when we're together. We know each other's secrets. Our love is deep. John is writing and teaching and I'm painting. We've always laughed together, and in the face of all this we still laugh and tease each other mercilessly.

We have good friends, and we travel a bit. Even though the fear is always there, deep, and we're struggling, in spite of all this we're happy. John and I are talkers, and as far as the lupus is concerned, this has been both our salvation and our downfall.

"We can't talk about this stuff all the time. It spirals us down. We just end up feeding each other's angst."

"I know. Let's go somewhere."

There have always been times in my life when I have felt these paradoxes simultaneously: great joy and great sorrow; great bravado and great hesitation; great strength and great vulnerability. It doesn't feel strange to me — the positive trying to lift the negative, the negative just as intent on dragging the positive down. It's just that I'm caught in the middle and feeling the pull of gravity from both sides.

March, 1979

I apply for a part-time position at the Topham Brown Public Art Gallery in Vernon as director/curator. Suddenly I have a job in the art world. The salary is a pittance, more of an honorarium really, but I'll be required to work a mere forty hours a month. With the help of a large team of volunteers, I'll be responsible for everything: arranging shows, hanging and displaying artwork, meeting with artists, hosting openings, unpacking and packaging crates of work, publicity, etc. It seems an amazing opportunity for a young artist and I'm thrilled.

I'm to put in my hours at my own discretion, and this is the key to my taking the job. If my fatigue or arthritis is bad, it will be possible to rearrange my work schedule. Just as importantly, this flexibility will allow me to continue to keep my secret a secret.

Most of the time, I manage well. I love the job. I start to regain some lost confidence. Some days though, events piggyback at the gallery and many things need to be done at once. I summon up the physical and mental strength and get these jobs done. Inside, I'm beginning to shut down, my muscles aching, joints flaming. Fatigue is pulling at my eyelids. My eyes feel dry and gritty, like I'm seeing the world through gauze. *Or smoke.*

When I finally can return home, I collapse on the bed and cry out of sheer frustration. I cannot accept this. I cannot accept this disease that offers up defeat after defeat. My mind cannot accept it. My soul cannot. *How can I carry on like this, day after day, year after year?* When I am this tired, I cannot bear to think of a whole life lived like this.

It never once occurs to me to tell someone connected with the gallery that I'm not feeling well or that I have lupus. I think that if for an instant I let down and reveal my illness, that will be it. I'll be defined as a sick person. People will avoid me or treat me like something precious. I can't risk that.

I also think that if I begin to let down, I'll fall apart. I'll be Humpty Dumpty falling off the Great Wall. I'll be the shell of an egg hitting hard ground, smashed into a thousand jagged-edged pieces: "And all the kings horses and all the kings men couldn't put Humpty Dumpty together again."

I think, *If I don't lose control, if I hold myself together tightly enough, I'll be defended. I'll be safe.*

~~~~

Many, many times over the years, I cross a room and put my head against John's chest. He wraps his arms around me, strokes my back and says softly, "OK, OK."

"*I'm so tired. I'm just so tired.*"

"*I know.*"

September, 1980

Knock, knock, knock! I open the door of our flat to a smiling delivery boy.

"Are you Jude Clarke?"

"Yes."

"Well, this is a delivery for you."

I'm looking at an unwrapped, brand-new Vilas rocking chair. "Oh, you must have the wrong person. That wouldn't be for me."

"But it is."

"But it *couldn't* be."

"Well, it *has* to be." We both laugh. "You'd better take it 'cause my boss isn't going to like me bringing it back to the store. He'll just send me back up here with it again."

"OK."

No note. No card. I place the chair in the middle of the living-room floor, settle into it, run my fingers over its smooth polished maple arms and begin to rock back and forth.

It turns out this is a no-occasion-necessary present for us from my mother and father. I can just hear Dad saying to Mom, "Those kids have got to have something more comfortable to sit on than those ridiculous lawn chairs they keep hauling all over the country." The fact that *he'd* like something more comfortable to sit on when he visits us is beside the point.

A few months later, when people ask me why we've decided to get married after "living in sin" all these years, I laugh and say, "It has something to do with a rocking chair, but really, it's because we love each other and want to celebrate that in a public way."

Spring, 1963 (age 8)

"Now bung it in and tamp it down really hard.
The roots need firm earth to hold on to. Like
this. See?"

I roll these new words around on my tongue.
"Bung! Tamp!"

"Now you do it . . . good! This bush is called a
Bleeding Heart and when I was a little girl your
age, your grandma took me out into the garden
on the farm and told me the story about the
Prince and the Princess."

"Tell it to me, Mom."

She plucks a pink, heart-shaped flower from a
string of hearts on the slender plant stem, gently
pulls the two outside petals apart and begins,
"Once upon a time . . . "

Climbing into bed that night, I discover a green,
cloth-covered book on my pillow. Its title is *The
Secret Garden*. I open it to the first page and am
soon lost in the story of a little girl who loses
both of her parents to cholera in Africa and is
sent to live with an uncle in England, an unfamiliar landscape. Lonely, she finds solace in the
discovery of a green and growing hidden
garden.

May 23, 1981

John and I are to be married in the garden of the home I grew up in, encircled by our two families and a few close friends. The garden is spring-bright with every colour of perennial, including my favourite Himalayan Primroses, and blooming throughout, dozens of tulips Mom and Dad had planted the fall before. Apparently, there are several clumps of white "fake" tulips too, which completely escape my notice. (A few days after the wedding, when I learn of their existence and respond with horror at the idea of anything artificial being part of my wedding day, Mom will say wryly, "Well, Jude, we couldn't get them all to bloom on exactly May 23rd, as you specified, and there were a few empty spots.")

Franny, Rhonda, and Dad and I are standing in the front yard, composing ourselves to walk around to the back garden. We've all got the jitters, but I'd say I'm the calmest, by far. My brother, Joe, suddenly appears around the corner of the house, yells, "Hang on, you guys" and runs across the street to ask the neighbour if he could turn off his lawnmower until later. "We've got a wedding going on over here! Thanks!"

Peter, our friend from Vancouver, pulls up the driveway in a taxi at the last minute, throws some bills at the driver, gives me his "dancing-eyes" grin and races around to the back to join the others.

I take Dad's arm and he asks, "Are you OK, honey?"

"I am Dad. I love you."

And off we go, our little procession of four, through the side gate and past the spot where Mom helped me plant my first pansy garden, past the filbert tree where I'd gathered nuts in the fall from the ground. The tree's no longer there but I can still feel the smooth dry surfaces of the filberts rolling in my hands.

We're walking over the slate path I'd bounced my India rubber ball on, and up the stone steps onto the upper lawn. Our friends and families are grouped together in the shade under the huge red maple tree. It was under this tree that my friends and I played "house design" in the fall, raking up piles of dark red leaves and then carefully dividing them up into layouts of narrow bands that would indicate the rooms of our "dream houses".

One winter, I'd made a skating rink under the same tree. I rushed home from school each day to hose another layer of water on the thin ice, working through dark with just the back-door light, until Mom called me in for supper. I didn't tell my friends about the rink until it was finished and then I invited them over, one-by-one, to skate after school.

~~~~

My father and I cross the green lawn towards the others. Dad and I embrace and as he moves away to join Mom, I look up into John's eyes, my heart beating. *It is you. It will always be you.*

~~~~

Dad had been worrying for the last month about serving alcohol — especially since there's to be an open bar — at our wedding dance. We're having the dinner and dance reception at the Kalamalka Lake Country Club for about eighty friends and relatives. The club is a modest, two-floor lodge my grandfather had helped establish and build with a group of friends in the thirties. Dad's worried about people driving into town along the winding lake road after they've been drinking.

We let him figure it out and he decides, "OK, we'll close the bar at midnight and then coffee will be served before anyone takes off."

The live band everyone is dancing to is The Lent Brothers, all the way from Edmonton and Vancouver, to play for our wedding. All five brothers, including John, are musicians: three play guitar, one drums, another stand-up bass, and they all sing. Their sister, Susan, joins them on stage. Susan sings in a choral group in Edmonton now, but she was a member of the folk-rock group The Circle Widens in Edmonton in the sixties. John, Harry and Susan had put the group together and had had the time of their lives playing gigs, throughout their university years. John would say to me, "You should have heard Susan singing Janis Joplin. She was incredible!" Marylou, the only sibling who doesn't play an instrument or sing (smart girl, somebody's got to be an original), is convinced to join them on stage, too.

~~~~

Joe and I are dancing to "Born to be Wild". He leans into me and says, "You're just great!"

"So are you!"

1970 (age 15)

Mom and Dad are seated at either end of the supper table. Joe and I are sitting kitty-corner as far away as possible from each other. Franny is away, travelling in Europe, and Len is in Vancouver finishing his pharmacy degree.

Joe gets this maniacal grin on his face and while Mom and Dad are concentrating on their food, catches my eye, starts tapping the side of his nose on the very spot a huge pimple is gracing my own nose. I'd been treating it with Noxema for a couple of days and instead of healing it, the cream has absorbed into and then expanded the zit into a festering, red volcano on the verge of pus-yellow eruption.

"Hey, Rudolf !" Joe mouths to me.

When I yell something back at him, Mom snaps, "All right, that's enough Joe, or I'll send you out to the kitchen with your dinner." This is a reference to the fact that in our pre-teenage years, Joe ate as many meals at the breadboard in the kitchen as he did in the dining room with the rest of us.

Now Mom is saying to Dad, "Reid, just let them fight. They'll be the best of friends when they grow up." My dad raises one eyebrow dubiously. Scowling at "my tormentor" I think, *yeah, right. That'll happen in a million years.*

~~~~

At midnight, I see Dad going over to the bartender. They're gesturing and talking over the roar of the music and the next thing I see, Dad's found Mom. He's scooping her up in his arms, and with a huge grin, waltzing her across the dance floor. John comes over and I ask, "What's up?"

"Your dad's having a really good time. He just told Gary to keep the bar open until 2:00 a.m. Then everybody's going to be served a lot of coffee before they go home."

August, 1981

I decide to leave the art gallery position because I haven't been making any art of my own and realize I won't be able to as long as I keep on working. I don't have the energy for both. Getting back to my own painting seems important now. I want to hold paintbrushes, dip them in paint, draw lines on paper again.

I've also begun to think about having children.

When I was small, I assumed I'd have children. It was what you did: you met a boy, married him after dating for a long time and then you had babies. Later, in high school, I still thought I'd have children, but *after* I'd gone to university, become an artist, dated a *lot* of boys and travelled the world.

Then I met John. He was the most exciting and dangerously handsome man I had ever met. I'd always been attracted to boys who were "trouble" and John didn't let me down in that department. He was "the one", though, and no one was more surprised than me that I'd found him at the age of nineteen.

We didn't discuss children for years, not because of my illness but because we were doing other things, moving around a lot, having a good time in spite of what the lupus was putting us through. When we finally did begin to, I was twenty-seven and had been living with lupus for seven years. A family wasn't going to be something that would just happen now, be the next natural step in the "grand adventure". Everything about it seemed infinitely complicated and fraught with peril. There were real concerns involving lupus and pregnancy. But women with lupus did have healthy pregnancies and healthy babies, too. All kinds of women with all kinds of health problems do go ahead and have babies, even knowing the risks. I didn't know if I possessed that kind of courage; a pregnancy for me would be especially risky because of my daily medications and kidney disease.

Late Spring, 1983

The wolf has gone too deep into the forest. Its darkness has only made her feel more alone. Now she wants to leave but each time she breaks through one maze of

tangled branches, there is another. It doesn't matter
which way she turns, there is always something blocking
her path. The ground slips beneath her. Ravenous and
lost, made crazy by fear, she turns on herself, splices her
own skin and with feral precision, rips open her own
heart.

John brings me home midway through the dinner
we've been having at a restaurant with his parents and
sister, here from Edmonton. I had started feeling ill at the
restaurant, panicky. At home, I'm leaning over the toilet
bowl, throwing up. My heart is beating too fast. John is
standing in the doorway. I can hardly look at him. When
I do, I can see he's had it. For the last month, I haven't
been able to sleep at night. John wakes every morning to
find me sitting on the couch, tense and exhausted. He's
teaching in Kelowna this year and it isn't until he leaves
for work each day that I finally fall asleep. He calls me late
in the afternoon to see if I'm all right. As soon as classes
are over, he rushes home. He's exhausted.

I tell him to go back to the restaurant and I apologize again and again. After he leaves, I can't get my body
to stop shuddering. I'm crying. I can't catch my breath.
I've been tormenting myself daily with the decision to
have children or not to have children. One glimpse of a
mother or father with a baby starts the questions, flashing
red neon in my brain,

Would I get sick? Could I physically care for a baby? Would
the drugs affect the baby? How could I possibly have the energy?
How badly would I torment myself about whether or not I was a

good enough mother? This is John's life too. If we don't have children what would I be depriving him of? If we do, what would I be shouldering him with?

On and on and on. Every way I look at it, I can only see myself failing. I'll be failing John if we don't have kids. If we do have them, I won't be able to be the kind of mother I'll want to be and then I'll be failing both John and myself. And the child. I believe in the end it'll be me, because I'm the one with the disease, who will direct our lives one way or the other, the one who will make the final, irreversible decision. I don't know if I can live with that. I feel there can be no peace for me, no acceptable resolution in my head, whichever way the decision goes.

John and I discuss all of this, over and over again. When he tells me he's not sure he wants me to go through a pregnancy, or that he was never sure, anyway, before he'd even met me, that he'd ever have children; that he loves me and having or not having children has nothing to do with that, I think he's being noble, or trying to protect me.

I've been going to other people's baby showers for ten years. I have a group of friends who had their babies young and another group who, like me, are thinking about or having children now, in their late twenties. But my friends don't have lupus. I go to their showers and smile, because I'm genuinely happy for them. I listen, hear their dreams, see the love on their faces as they cuddle, nurse and coo secrets to these new little souls. Then I come home and cry — to John, to my sister, to myself in the middle of the night when I can't sleep.

We go to Vancouver to talk to my nephrologist. He lays out the risks and I tell him how hard it's been for me to make this decision, that I still haven't made it. My doctor looks at me directly then and says, "I don't think you should go through a pregnancy. I think you'll flare and your kidneys will be involved."

My worries are legitimate, my fears real. Hearing this from my doctor validates everything I've been feeling. Later, when we leave his office, John tells me he feels relief; he has always been more concerned with the risk of me having a child than the idea of a life without a child. I finally believe him. We look at the life we already have.

It is the concrete act of finally making the decision that saves me. It's the indecision, the constant berating of myself that's been doing me in. In my heart, I think I've been preparing for the eventuality of a life without children for a long time. I've already mourned the absence of a child in my life, have felt that sorrow because I've played out the possibility a hundred times over in my head.

This soft sphere of sadness — the realization that John and I will never have a child together — begins to lift and beneath it is the simple truth that for the eight years we've been together, John and I have been happy. We begin to see that we are our own complete, however small, family.

We decide too that we can't carry the weight of the disease alone any longer. The lupus isn't killing me, but my soldiering on, pretending that everything is all right, is. I've become afraid to set up appointments, to accept social invitations. I worry I'll have to cancel at the last minute, or worse, go, and pretend I'm not in pain or exhausted. And John. He runs interference for me. He's the one who comes up with excuses, tells people I'm out when I'm sleeping. This is the only way we know how to cope. This is the way we'd seen our parents cope. We carry on like this until, thankfully, we can't do it anymore.

Now I start talking to friends, telling them what we've been struggling with. Each time I confide in someone, some of the weight of it lifts. I gain a "new world". I discover people do know I have the disease or at least know something is wrong with me, but since I never mention it, they feel they can't. Invariably, these friends respond to my new directness by confiding in me a struggle in their own lives. My friendships become honest again. My life changes. I begin to feel connected to people and the world again.

Everything begins to change. I haven't had a kidney flare in four years, since the very first one. We begin to make plans with new hope. I'm twenty-eight and John is thirty-five. John has a full-time, permanent position at the college. We buy a small, old house with a bay window and dark wood wainscoting. We paint two rooms white — a studio for me and an office for John. John lines one wall of his office with shelves and fills them with his books. He builds himself a desk and a larger painting table for me and we plant flower gardens all around the house.

John finds an Old English Sheepdog breeder in Edmonton and the puppy we choose arrives by plane one day. We can see a carrier table with a large white container on it being wheeled over the airport tarmac. The container has one-inch round holes all over it and out of each sprouts a large white clump of puppy hair. She hangs over my shoulder the whole drive home and we name her Georgia.

The wolf has finally broken free of the forest and is now standing at the edge looking down into a valley. She wants to cross to the other side, but she can sense fire smoldering, hidden beneath tall grasses in open fields. She must be patient. It is only when evening falls that she can step safely out into the open. The danger fades with the setting of the sun.

April, 1984

It's a perfect spring evening, still light out and still warm. I'm walking down the sidewalk to the corner store to buy milk. The cement is dry and crumbling in spots where salt had been dumped on the winter ice. Georgia's snuffling along ahead of me, turning around to check once in a while to make sure I'm still with her.

John has just had his third book accepted and the publishers are going to use one of my paintings on the cover.

There are crocuses pushing their way through the earth under a lilac tree. The grass is spring green.

Earlier today, I visited my sister and her just-born baby boy. Jonathon's little face is serious, and when my sister talks to him, his eyes gaze intently into hers. When she lifts him up and lays him in my arms, his fingers curl, like the petals of a flower, around mine.

August, 1984

"Honey, come on out back, before you leave."

I follow him through the garage lined with rakes and hoes and ladders and clippers. We stop briefly and he removes a small cutting tool from a meticulously organized shelf. We walk through the end door and out into the back garden. He stops on the slate path and takes two long steps into the tangle of colour. He reaches between the blue asters and red lilies and white shasta daisies and makes a small motion with his hand.

My father turns to face me and offers me a single, yellow-petalled rose. And his shy grin. A rose and a grin. Perfect.

November 1984

Wolf doesn't leave me in peace for long. He finds me again. And again.

I'm downtown, helping my mother choose a painting frame, when I feel a sudden, stabbing pain in my stomach. I make it to the car, then vomit all over the front seat. John meets us at the hospital. Dr. McAvoy brings in a surgeon to examine me and they leave my bedside to confer. Later, I have exploratory surgery and when I wake up, learn my appendix has been removed.

One month later, we are in the neighbouring town having a quiet New Year's Eve with Ian and Rhonda. Just after midnight, I become aware of a strange sensation in my feet. Reaching down, I pull up a leg of my jeans, pull off my sock and see that my ankle and the top of my foot are swollen. My foot looks like a loaf of unbaked bread. The skin feels tight. *I'm flaring. It's my kidneys.* The next day, Dr. McAvoy explains to me that it's most likely my immune system has been triggered by the physical trauma of the appendectomy. This is a response typical of lupus. In my case, the antibodies have mistaken my own kidneys for the enemy. *Friendly fire.*

I begin steroid treatment immediately. Dark images of the upcoming months race through my mind. *I have no power here.* I'd been feeling so well in the summer. I'd resolved so many things and now I'm painting, looking forward to and preparing for an exhibition with two other local artists in the fall.

~~~~

When I'm feeling strong enough, my father and I go on walks together. I love this time with him. We walk through the old neighbourhood, gossiping about relatives and other people. Dad has an irreverent side to him. He blurts out witty, surprising things and we both laugh.

One day, I tell him about the physical tension I still feel, the kind I know he's felt most of his life, and how the occasional anxiety attack will scare me.

Dad asks, "What is it that scares you?"

We're walking up a steep hill, both puffing a little. I shrug, a little embarrassed, and say, "I guess, it's just that I think I might faint, or even die or something."

Dad puts his hand on my elbow, we both stop and he says in a reassuring tone of voice, "Well, you can be sure you're not going to die from anxiety, even though it feels like it, and that if you do faint, you'll come to again. This is what I do."

I'm listening carefully because I know Dad knows what I'm talking about.

Now my practical pharmacist father is saying, "I become aware of my clenched hands, zero in on that and then lightly shake them for a minute. A few minutes later, I become aware they're clenched again and so I keep repeating the shaking process until I feel more relaxed."

I look to see if he's teasing. *He's serious.* "Really? Does it work?"

"Well . . . sometimes. And then sometimes it doesn't do a damn thing," he snorts. We carry on, trudging up the hill towards Black Rock.

~~~~

One day my father tells me this story, the only one I can ever recall him telling me that was about *his* father.

"You wouldn't believe some of the quacks who used to come into the drugstore, claiming miracle cures. This will cure *this*. This will cure *that*. One time, I was at the back of the pharmacy crouched down stacking shelves — I was probably about sixteen at the time — and your grandfather was standing at the dispensary counter. I could hear someone say, "I don't know what's wrong with me, but look at my skin, it's orange!" After a few cautious questions, your grandfather finds out the old guy has been drinking about a gallon of carrot juice every day, to make himself healthier or have more energy or something, and the carrots have turned him the colour of pumpkin! I didn't dare straighten up and go see because I was already trying to stifle my laughter, as it was. I probably would have exploded if I got a look at him."

Dad takes off his hat and slaps it against his trousers as he delivers the next line, "My father's advice was, 'I'd stop drinking that carrot juice if I were you and see if it clears up.' He said it with a completely straight tone of voice. Your grandfather wasn't a humorous man, but we sure laughed that day."

Late January, 1985

Dad hasn't suffered a manic-depressive episode since he'd been put on lithium ten years ago. Lately though, he's been tiring easily and generally feeling unwell. His doctor has put it down to several minor things. Then he has an ECG and discovers, alarmingly, that he needs a triple bypass. He is scheduled to have the operation on Valentine's Day at a hospital in Vancouver.

John and I go to the Vernon hospital the morning of the day he's being flown to the coast. "Now, don't tease the nurses too much, Dad."

Walking away, walking down the hall, I resist the urge to turn around and say, "See you, take care, I love you," one more time.

The day after his operation, after we'd been informed of its success, I'm downtown doing errands. I stop in at Boots Drugstore to say hello to my brother. I reach the pharmacy and here's Len walking out from behind the counter, taking me in his arms, saying, "Dad died, Jude."

I'm not hearing this. I'm sobbing. Len takes me home and sits with me, keeps saying, "I love you, Jude." Now my brother Joe is parking his car. He's walking across the road to our house, slowly, carrying a bottle of rye. Len has reached John at the college and now he's here, too. Len leaves for the airport. He has to get to Vancouver, to bring Mom and Franny home. Thankfully, my sister is with Mom. Franny's husband, Don, arrives from work. Len's wife, Sharon, makes dinner for everyone. Later, around nine in the evening, Len and Mom and Franny finally come through the door, their grief rolling in waves with them. Everything is happening in slow motion.

My gentle father, with dry wit and sensitive soul, this complicated man who loves his family with such simple ease, is gone.

We bury him in the old Coldstream Cemetery, where pine trees shade the graves and cows graze the perimeter. He is seventy years old. My mother is too young to lose him. I am too young to lose him.

There are wolves everywhere out there. I can't keep track of them. I draw an imaginary barricade around my family and wish none of them would step out of the enclosure. This way, I think I can keep them safe.

The flare goes on and on throughout summer and into fall. It's finally brought under control and I begin the long recovery process — getting the drugs out of my system and making my way out of a fatigue and sadness that are two-fold.

Sharon and Len had told my father, the day before he went to Vancouver for surgery, that Sharon was pregnant with his second grandchild. Their baby is born in September, Dad's birth month, too, and they name him Reid Michael Clarke.

John wrote this poem in memory of my father after he died:

"Artifice of Eternity"
for Reid M. Clarke (1914 to 1985)

we visit your grave tonight
its freshness heaved between
the weathered cement borders
of other older gravesites
under a pearling sky so pink
we think it is coincidence
something you might have arranged

the quiet of this place is loud
with other quiets   I listen
leave her kneeling above you
walk instead among the pines

they sway and crack to the wind
comfort your daughter my wife
who sits beside you in the mist
talks in the tongue you shared

you a polyphony of quiet anyway
sitting in the livingroom with your drink
speaking occasionally   listening

I respected you
old man refined into your forevers
am reminded of you wherever I look
your many instructions out at the cabin
your thirst for order now diminishing
in your absences

none of the rest of us can keep up
your quiet meticulous ways
your bewilderment over our times
your obsessions for innocence

I peer from the far corner of the cemetery
see her sitting there accompanying your mysteries
crouched between the cement and the granite now
        whispering

Yeats wished he might become a golden bird
I this love that seals your burial:

the refinement of her hand as it brushes
the crumbing granular soil above you

comforts you in this dusk

February 15, 1999

Mom and I visited Dad's grave today. We're going to plant some bulbs again next fall even though they don't do as well as the ground covers seem to. Dad loved spring bulbs. Finnegan had a grand time running free in the snow and managed to get caught on a barb-wire fence. She looked surprised and then affronted when we had to untangle her. She left behind a small tuft of toffee-coloured hair.

August, 1985

I can hear John's voice calling me back to shore. But I keep swimming, on the stormiest of days, out, out to the last yellow buoy, triumphant.

My right arm arcs out of the warm water, into the cooler air, and then slices down into the water again. My left arm draws up, arcs out of the water and into the air. Slices down into the water again. Arc. Dip. Arc. Dip. I keep my rhythm steady against the dissonance of the waves, the thundering sky.

Wolf is far, far away, on another shore.

It is only when I swim back and can see John's face that I am ashamed.

~~~~

John is the oldest son in a family of seven children. He grew up with illness in his family, too, his father's alcoholism. But that's John's story and his story to tell.

When I became ill, he thought it was his responsibility to hold everything together. He thought he knew exactly how to take care of me. To make me happy. He would just stuff his own feelings far inside and make things as easy and as fun as possible for me. He was good at that, used to doing it. I would say, "You have to let me do things for you. Do you know how hard it is, sometimes, to just *do that?* You take care of everything. I can't break through your self-sufficiency."

There was something John could do for himself. He could drink. He had always loved drinking and it had always been a problem in our life together. He was never cruel or even unkind to me, but the person that he really was would slip away and a stranger would take his place. The morning after, we always talked about how we each felt, in the same way we discussed everything else. I couldn't stand to see him so disappointed in himself. He knew how much his drinking upset me. I believe it was our acknowledgement of each other's hurt that made it possible for us to find our way back to one another, time and time again.

Sometimes I would worry, *I have caused or my disease has caused him to drink more.* Other times I felt that his having to cope with my lupus was no worse than my having to cope with his drinking. Or else, angry, *He can stop drinking. I can't stop having lupus.* Sometimes I would think that the burden of these two diseases could at least balance if not wipe each other out. *Not a chance.* I knew that the lupus was more terrible for him because there was nothing I could give up that would remove it from my life, let alone his.

~~~~

One night John goes to my mom's and visits with her and my sister late into the night. He disappears every ten minutes or so to the front hall to get something from his packsack. When he returns, he's a little bit drunker, a little bit sloppier. At first he's funny, then sarcastic, and then in tears. He passes out.

The next morning, faced with Mom's worried, questioning eyes, he asks if it would be all right if he went out and stayed at the cabin for awhile to think things through.

Hearing we're in trouble, one of John's brothers calls, "Just thought I'd come out and see you both this weekend." Our friend Peter phones from Vancouver, and when I tell him that John's at the cabin and that everything is all right, he doesn't believe me. He thinks I'm not admitting to him our world has fallen apart. Our world *has* fallen apart but in a way that's going to make it possible for John to feel better.

Once again, the cabin on Kalamalka Lake becomes a haven, a place for John to have some solitude. He walks from the cabin to the corner store every day and uses the pay phone to call me. Some evenings I drive out and we walk along the edge of the lake or through apple orchards. He's angry. Really angry. He says, "I'm not going to stop drinking for you, Jude. I'm not going to do this for anybody else, except me. I'm doing it for me. All my life I've been looking after people, pleasing them.

Making everything all right. Fuck 'em. I'm tired. I don't want to do that any more."

Spring, 1987

John is standing in the bedroom doorway. I'm slumped over, sitting on the bed. His voice is ragged with pain, "What am I supposed to do with all of this? Who can I talk to about the lupus? I'm caught every way I turn. If I even *hint* at my own frustrations, it upsets you. If I say anything about how the lupus makes *me* feel, you take it on as your own guilt and then I feel like I can't say anything. Can't you see how selfish that is? How unfair?"

I look up at him.

Yes. Yes, I can. But how can it not upset me? I have been the cause of all this. You didn't choose this life. You had pledged your love before any of this began. But I didn't see how impossible I was making it for you to express your own feelings. Yes. The very least I can do for you is listen to you without bringing up my own guilt. I can just listen.

Standing up, walking over and putting my arms around John, I whisper, "Yes. Yes, I can. I'm so sorry."

October, 1987, "Grey Ditch"

I'm sitting on a rock looking out over the valley. Georgia is beside me and no one else is around. I can see bits of two of the three valley lakes, Swan and Okanagan, in the distance. All the smells are familiar, as is the dryness of the autumn air. The raw umber, burnt sienna and yellow ochre of wild grasses warm the landscape, the benevolent, grey sky. *I can "get" that sky by mixing a little Sap green with Payne's grey and a lot of water.* There's a low buzzing in the air, the sound of lazy fall flies. It's different here than when I was a child, though. There's a well-kept walking path now and a bench at the top of the hill. It's still a great place to let your dog run free.

There are fewer orchards quilting the valley landscape. Just below me, there's an old tree that's been left untouched for years. Its crooked branches still hold a few apples. *They'd probably taste delicious even though they're wormy.*

I've come up here early, to have some time to myself and think things over. A lot has happened in the last four years. They've been the hardest years of my life, but in the end, I've come to a place of grace. Much has been resolved. I've faced so many changes, made so many decisions, grieved so many events beyond my control, accepted these same events, and in the end come out a stronger person. *What's that?* I hear a rustle in a clump of tall grass a fair distance to the right of me. Georgia's head lifts, alert. *No. Nothing. Nothing's there.*

I'm not as worried about John. He's been getting some help and is beginning to feel better. He's not drinking. This year away is a godsend for both of us.

Wait! There it is again. I stand up this time and walk a few yards, Georgia following, towards the spot the noise is coming from. I scan the whole area but still can't see anything. "Georgia, there's nothing there." We return to my rock.

I've recovered from the appendectomy and kidney flare, tapered off the high-dose steroids, and am finally back to my usual maintenance dose. I've lost weight and my muscles are strong again. I'm even looking forward to doing some cross-country skiing before we leave.

I lean over and untie the lace of one of my boots, shake a small stone out, pull up my sock, put the boot back on and retie the lace. There are a few more clouds rolling in from the west now. We may be in for a small storm. Georgia is restless.

We had the family burial service for Dad at the cemetery in August. Afterwards, we'd all gone out to the cabin so we could be "with" Dad. We were quiet looking out at the lake, each of us lost in our own thoughts. Looking around, I could see the touch of my father's hand from the summer before, everywhere: the newly-painted lattice work on the bottom half of the cabin, the new piece of indoor/outdoor covering the steps, and the freshly-oiled cedar chairs. The red canoe was tipped over under the willow tree, waiting to be fixed. A piece of the metal edging needed to be replaced. It was hanging from the side of the canoe and looked out of place. By this time, late summer, Dad would have attended to it, got rid of the sharp, rusty piece of metal — the potential danger to a child's bare foot and the consequent sure "ruin" of that child's summer.

So much has happened and changed in the fifty years since Dad bought the cabin, and yet, so much is the same: the seasonal rituals, the faded photographs taped to the back of the kitchen cabinet, the world's "ugliest green ashtray" still sitting on the window ledge. Mom and Dad had picked it up in the States on their honeymoon. In Las Vegas, I think. Even the turquoise Melmac dishes are the same ones I used as a child. I wouldn't be at all startled if Dad walked down the path just now, whistling and glad to see his family. *If only.*

I feel the first drops of rain on my skin. Standing, I rough up Georgia's head, "Good dog!", and turn to head back up the path to the car. Something moves in the periphery of my vision. I turn to face it directly but it's gone. There's nothing there.

"Come on, Georgia, let's go!" Georgia bounds ahead of me, looking forward now to the treat she knows is waiting in the car for her.

Fall, 1986

JOHN HAS BEEN GRANTED A TWELVE-MONTH SABBATICAL to
write. He can go anywhere in the world, and after a few
recommendations from other writers, he chooses
Strasbourg, France.

Neither of us has been to Europe. We don't know a
soul in France, speak only high-school French, and of
course, there is the lupus. But neither of us have a
moment's hesitation about going. We can't wait. Paradox,
again.

People ask me, "Aren't you afraid to go, with your
disease?" "How can you?" My response is "How can I not?
We've been offered this grand adventure. I'm going to
live my life."

We organize the details carefully. Before we leave
Canada, I contact a doctor in Strasbourg, an immunologist, who agrees to monitor the lupus. My internist here
in Vernon, Dr. McAvoy, gives me a copy of my medical file

and letters detailing my medical history, and especially, the report of my renal involvement from Dr. Ballard in Vancouver.

I pack enough medication for six months. Several people tell me, "Make sure you get a letter from your doctor that says lupus isn't contagious and explains why you're carrying all those pills. Otherwise you may have trouble at customs." They freak us out so much that by the time John and I are standing in the airport security line-up, we're sure we're going to be prevented from leaving the country and arrested for *something*. I glance over at John. *He certainly looks guilty.*

Our turn. John goes first, and after the metal detector indicates "all clear" and nothing dangerous found in his carry-on bag, is waved through. *Great. So* he's *in.* I step up, readying myself for the inevitable. As the security person is opening my bag, I start blabbering explanations for the pills. She looks up at me, says blandly, "carry on," and I'm through. It's almost a disappointment.

January 1, 1988

We arrive by train in the middle of the night. The hotel concierge listens patiently to our faltering French and makes a phone call. We can tell he's had a lot to drink. The ferry ride from Dover to Calais, our stomachs roiling with the great brown sea-waves, and the long train ride from Dover to Strasbourg have left us still excited, but tired, too, and a little vulnerable.

Like bewitched children following the piper, we're willing to do whatever we're told. The concierge motions to follow him and out we go back into the night. We walk alongside the dark ribbon of a canal and turn a corner into an even darker alleyway. It dawns on both of us, too late, that we could easily be mugged, but a door opens, and suddenly we are in a small cafe full of people and noise and light. It's like an impossibly bold Van Gogh painting cracking open in three dimensions, the air thick with laughter, music, and the spicy aroma of pizza.

The concierge nods to the woman who lays before us a complete Alsatian feast. We babble gratefully, *"Merci beaucoup, Madame! Merci beaucoup, Monsieur!"* They exchange a small smile and bid us, *"Bon Appetit, Madame et Monsieur."*

We look at each other and burst into helpless laughter. We have arrived.

~~~~

The next morning, we have croissants and coffee in the hotel dining room then head out into the street. We know there's a famous cathedral here but we're not sure where it's located. We walk along the quays which edge the canals, see barges anchored and moving, and white swans floating in the murky water. There is the smell of stagnant water. Half-timbered houses lean haphazardly into one another. We stop at a footbridge, wait while it's lifted with a manual crank and watch a boat pass through.

We have arrived the year Strasbourg is celebrating its 2,000th birthday.

As the bridge is lowered, I turn to John, throw my arms around him and kiss him. "Yeah," he grins, "this is all right."

We turn towards the city centre and walk along crowded streets. Making slow progress down a narrow cobblestone street that is closed to cars but holds a throng of people *and* their dogs, John suddenly stops. "Wow." He points upward. I look up and see a massive spire. We make a turn and walk into a huge open square. Sitting in the middle of it, like some great prehistoric beast, is "the Cathedral". It's made of stone and is a complexity of peaks, wings, stained-glass windows, gargoyles and intricate friezes. The exterior is reddish brown, aged by weather and the soot of thousands of years of river commerce — the Rhine edges the city. There is scaffolding laced over several areas. The cathedral was designed to have twin spires but the second one was never completed. The whole thing is . . . *overwhelming.*

A few days after our arrival, we find a phone booth in a busy square, at the hub of the medieval district near the famous restaurant called Maison des Tanneurs. I call Dr. Laporte from the pay phone and arrange to meet him the next day, at the hospital where he has his practice. I see him four times throughout the year. I have gone from being afraid to ask anything about my disease to wanting to know as much as possible. The more information I have, the more I relax. It's a wonderful chance for me to ask questions of a doctor engaged in immunology research. He confirms the medical treatment I've been receiving in

Canada has been the best, the most up-to-date. I hadn't doubted that. It's just good to hear it from another source.

Early January, 1988

John presses the outside intercom button.

I whisper quickly, "Don't forget to call her *Madame* Vauthier. The French expect that. They're more formal than us."

John flashes me a look — Since when did you know so much about the French — then we hear a melodic trill, *"Bonjour?"*

"Bonjour Madame Vauthier. C'est John Lent et Jude Clarke, ici." The door to the apartment opens to a tall, dark-haired woman with twinkling eyes.

In time, Simone adopts us. She takes us to the country for *tarte flambe.* She has us for lunch a couple of times a week and introduces us to Christiane, Malcolm and Pierre and Marie-Yvette. She and John talk about Canadian Literature, and writing and teaching and other writers. They trade stories, gossipy, funny descriptions of English department politics that have us all laughing.

Late January, 1988

Every morning John goes down to the *patisserie* below our two-room apartment in La Petite France, the medieval district of Strasbourg, and brings back still-warm almond croissants for breakfast. We eat them at the arborite and metal-legged table we've put together in the larger room, and, after brushing away the flaky crumbs, we relocate the table to the kitchen where it's transformed into John's writing desk. Once the desk is set up, we can't get by to use the bathroom, get anything from the two-foot square fridge, use the hot plate or leave the apartment without dismantling the whole thing. So we get the ritual down to a science, and after a week wonder how we could possibly have needed all the "stuff" and "space" we'd had back in Vernon.

We purchase a foamy for our bed and place it in a corner of the big room alongside four wall-shelves. We put together a longer, larger version of his desk for me under the two huge windows that open inward. My view is of a little enclosed courtyard that contains two slender trees and several pigeons. From the beginning, the pigeons are curious and come right up to the ledge. They poke their heads through the open windows, coo and cock these heads quizzically.

But the real drama is going on in the flat next to ours. It faces the courtyard too, at a right angle, and I have a full view of the occupant's entrance. Each day, a woman arrives just after noon. A few minutes later, a man arrives. Time passes . . . the woman leaves a few minutes before the man. They know I'm here, that I probably realize why they're there, and I make up all kinds of stories in my head about the other lives they lead, away from these clandestine rendezvous.

~~~~

From the moment John starts writing, he's off and running. All I can hear on the other side of the wall is industry, industry, industry. He's rented an electric typewriter for the year and his ideas are just pouring out. Clackity, clackity, clack, clack.

I'm sitting on the other side of the wall, looking at a full sheet of pristine white Arches watercolour paper. I don't have a clue where to begin. I fiddle around for a few days mixing a new palette and drawing a bit. On the third day I can't stand it anymore and call around the corner, "Are you having a good time out there? It certainly sounds like it. As you probably know, I'm *really* happy for you."

Smug laugh from the kitchen, "It'll come Jude. It'll come. Now, be quiet. I'm working!"

My first painting is of three pigeons sitting on the window ledge, looking at me.

~~~~

This new landscape poses a real challenge to me. Until now I'd painted a rural Okanagan landscape. As always, I gravitate to water, strolling alongside the numerous interconnecting canals. But this water is different — strangely still and foul-smelling.

> *The wolf is immediately intrigued. She will never swim in these waters but she will return to them again and again in her mind when fire strikes again.*

I stop often to look at the houses edging the opposite sides of the canals. They simply drop into the water.

Several have a small boat tied next to a door. The reflections of the buildings change from day to day, sometimes from hour to hour, depending on the quality of light. Some days, they're airy and the buildings float lightly, upside down, on the water. Other days, there are no reflections. The water is opaque and the buildings seem held up by a solid dark mass. Space is contained, water motionless.

I'm drawn to the buildings' forms, the rough, crumbling textures of their surfaces, and the gap-toothed horizon line they make against the always shifting, low sky. I see these urban landscapes as blocks of colour, as interconnecting shapes of sky, buildings, and water.

I have found my subject and now work begins for me, too.

A few years before, I had switched from using oil to watercolour paints. At school, I'd been told that Serious Artists didn't paint with watercolour and two instructors, obviously scornful of the medium, succeeded in discouraging my interest. *(Where do these people come from and why do they become teachers?)* Once I finished school and was free of their judgements, I went out and bought some watercolour paints and brushes. The first time I put a fully-loaded brush to wet paper, I realized with a physical rush that I had found my medium. The paint pooled across the paper, suggesting atmosphere and transparent depth with each new wash. Mystery. There was an elusive quality to the paint itself; it didn't want to be pinned down. Paintings that I considered complete seemed to stop shy of a firm resolution. I liked that. Ambiguity. When I drew lines with either fine or fat paintbrushes, their edges would soften, absorb into the wet paper. If I wanted more distinct lines, I could apply them to dryer paper. Endless possibility stretched before me. *This is a language I want to learn.*

~~~~

I saturate the paper with water, brush several more strokes of clear water over its surface. Bending down and looking at the paper sideways, I can see the water sits like a thick film on its surface. *It's ready.* I draw a few quick, strong lines with a watercolour pencil. These pencils are great because they're hard and don't dissipate on the paper like watercolour paint does. A line remains a line. I begin filling in the geometric shapes I've made with washes of paint, keep working slowly, adding more pigment as the painting drys until an image forms. I brush the space around the image until I'm satisfied with the movement, the feel of it. Then I wait. The trick is to be able to know when the paper is dry enough to add more paint. I want the image to still appear to float on the paper so it can't be too dry. It's something you have to intuit and the only way you can learn how to do that is by painting a lot.

~~~~

My first successful painting is of a church called St. Thomas at the end of our street. I paint it as a dreamy, floating structure that fills the sheet of paper. Now, when I look at my work from that year, it seems to me I was viewing Strasbourg through rose-coloured glasses. I think

Figure 3
Eglise St. Thomas, 1988
Watercolour

the palette I chose to paint in was based more on my psychological state of mind at the time than on an actual representation of the urban landscape before me.

~~~~

We work through the mornings, then John leaves the flat ahead of me. I join him later at his favourite cafe, Le Palais de la Glace, by the Cathedral, and we sit and watch the crowds streaming by. We're especially curious about the gypsies, who teach their children to beg, play instruments, and dance for the tourists. It's a business venture. Nothing sentimental about it.

We explore new areas of the city and eat salty, soft pretzels stuffed with cream cheese as we walk over the cobblestone streets back to our apartment. We always go home carrying an unwrapped baguette, and once a week, a bouquet of fresh-cut flowers we've bought from one of the street vendors for our dining/writing table. We have a late lunch and top it off with some delectable treat from one of the myriad *patisseries*.

Strasbourg is the unofficial dessert capital of Europe. We peer into *patisserie* windows, ogling the intricate concoctions — works of art, really — and each day, buy something different to taste. Each business has its own version of many of the same pastries and we soon discover which place makes the lightest *milles filles*, the thinnest, crispest florentines, the tastiest pine nut and vanilla cream cakes. No distance is too far to walk to the *cremerie* with the best and most varied cheeses, no *boulangerie* too out of the way for the terrines which reveal the most beautiful patterns of cooked ham or pork studded with green olives and pimentos, hard-boiled eggs, and tiny white onions when sliced. We laugh at the decadence of it all and because we walk miles every day, we don't even gain weight.

This entire year, I'm asymptomatic. I rarely have a headache, and only think about the lupus when we're trying to avoid the sun or I have my three-month checkup with Dr. Laporte. I still cope with daily fatigue but I had learned how to relax and sleep in the afternoons by the time we'd left for France.

John hasn't had a drink for almost a year (and still hasn't, as I write this book fourteen years later). This year is a gift for John. It's giving him the chance to regain his own health in a different place, away from old haunts and familiar patterns. He has no phone, no meetings to attend, no classes, nothing pressing. Most often, our biggest decision involves what we'll be eating for dinner or what place we'll explore next. There are no complicated work or personal relationships to balance. We realize our only responsibility is to look out for each other and our only expectation of the year is to write and paint. This is a writer and painters' Paradise.

This is Paradise to a person who lives with lupus.

May 1988

John has been invited to read his work at an international writers' conference in Paris. We take the train and settle into our hotel across the Seine from the Louvre. In the evening, we walk the few blocks to the Canadian Embassy for the wine and cheese reception, where we meet the other writers. John quickly finds a similar sensibility in his fellow Canadian writer, Gérald Godin. They leave the room to have a smoke together in the lobby — I can hear John's raucous laugh from where I'm standing looking at a painting on the wall.

Afterwards, returning to the hotel, we're hungry and ask the English-speaking proprietor if there's someplace nearby where we could get some food. "Yes," she says, "in St. Germain" and gives us directions. Once again, we find ourselves walking along unfamiliar streets in the dark, wondering if we should be doing this. We're about to go back, but turn a final corner and are drawn suddenly into a square full of people and noise and light.

The square is lined with at least three hundred small chairs placed outside the cafes and facing the square's centre. There are as many people sitting behind small tables, drinking wine or coffee. There's just a tiny space between each chair, so friends and strangers sit closely, side by side. The scene is lit with street lamps, lights from the cafés, and candles on the tables. We flop down into two empty seats.

I'm speechless. There's a vitality emanating from all the people; it's jumping around us and my heart is thumping. The young boy and girl to the left of me are animated and gesticulate as they talk. The boy keeps leaning into the girl, nuzzling her ear, stroking her hair. Just in front of me under a chair is, cliché of all clichés, a French poodle. He's unfazed by the carnival atmosphere, sleeping soundly. His mistress reaches down with an immaculately manicured hand and adjusts the blue ribbons on his ears. Coming from the small church across the square are the sounds of a violin. I look over to see not one but two violinists standing on the church steps, playing for the crowd. I listen for a while and then look up at the indigo sky. There, looking down on me, with a bandaged ear and woeful eyes, is Vincent Van Gogh, his self-portrait on a huge poster advertising an exhibition of his work.

Poor Vincent. He must have sat in this square. Maybe he sat with another artist or his brother Theo. I hope he wasn't alone.

I look over at John. *I wonder what's going on in your head, where you are right now and wonder, too, How is it that all of this came to me?*

~~~~

The next evening, we walk to the Georges Pompidou Centre where John and the other writers read their work. When several read in their native language, I have to content myself with listening to the cadence of their voices and the rhythm of their lines. It's interesting actually — more like hearing a piece of music spoken. Afterwards, we join a group for dinner, and later still, walk one of the women back to her hotel. The three of us pause for a minute on a bridge crossing the Seine. Twinkling lights from buildings and boats reflect and bob in the dark water on either side of us. We can see the Eiffel Tower.

For a minute, I stand suspended in time — bits of history and artists' names and their paintings pop into my mind. I feel like Bert, the chimneysweep in *Mary Poppins*, stepping through the painting canvas.

I'm inside the painting now. There's Pierre Auguste Renoir walking away from us. I can just see his burly back. I know where he's going. Home. To his happy family, his wife and children, where they live on the other side of the Louvre.

~~~~

In the upstairs flat beside our apartment, above the Creperie, an older woman leans out her window, calls down and chats to people going by. She stares silently at us each time we go in and out of our building. John always gives her a smile and says, *"Bonjour, Madame."* She never replies or smiles. John tells me, "I'm going to get her to smile at me before we leave France!"

One night, we're coming home late from a short trip to Basel. Driving down the street beside the Ill Canal, we notice it's populated with women in short skirts, grouped together or standing alone, dressed to kill. Suddenly, I spot our neighbour standing with the woman she lives with. These two women aren't young — in their late fifties I'd guess. But the French have a whole different approach to sexuality and age is not a factor. When I realize what I'm seeing, I exclaim, "John! Our neighbour is a hooker! She probably thinks you want more than a smile from her!"

THE LANGUAGE OF WATER

John is incredulous. He laughs at himself and the irony of the conquest he's taken on. He still vows to get a smile out of her before we leave France.

June 1988

Malcolm and Pierre, Simone, John and I drive out to Woert, a little town famous in France because it has the only restaurant in the whole country that doesn't serve alcohol. The restaurant is also famous for its food. We don't order from a menu; the meal is whatever they're serving that day. We have mixed greens picked from the garden behind the restaurant, pork roast and mushrooms in a savory sauce, mashed potatoes, very Alsatian. The feast is topped off with the restaurant's renowned meringue; it is ten inches high, light as air, and filled with homemade strawberry ice cream.

Afterwards, we go to Malcolm and Pierre's nearby summer cottage and meet some of their friends. Simone and I sit at the back of the house where there's heavy shade while the others stroll through the neighbourhood, looking at the half-timbered cottages, the abundant vegetable and flower gardens.

~~~~

Later, driving home to Strasbourg and lulled by the food and the warm, lazy afternoon, we all share confidences. I try to explain what lupus is, and once again am struck by the strangeness of the disease and its multi-faceted nature — the depths it takes me to, and the surfaces it allows me to break through — the active periods and the quiet ones when the disease is in remission, my own role in all of this and the unsolvable puzzle it is to me.

~~~~

Each day, John and I talk about our writing and painting. When I was eighteen and taking his first-year literature class, John's lectures filled my head with ideas and made me laugh, too. He was fresh from graduate studies at York University and in his own words "stuffed to the gills with that old grad-school virus of arrogance and superiority. I thought I knew everything."

I thought he did, too.

In the first week of class, he used words like micro and macrocosm and the phrase "stream of consciousness" as if we had been using them every day of our lives. Surreptitiously looking around the room, my suspicions were confirmed. *Everyone else looks like they know what he's talking about. Great.*

Extremely shy, I couldn't bring myself to speak up in class. If he called on me, and he had an annoying habit of doing this, I could feel myself flush and I'd choke out three or four words, never remembering what I'd said afterwards. Near the end of term, knowing I was an art student, John asked if I could prepare and give the class a short seminar that would explore the concept, "art for art's sake". Blushing, I said, "sure", already trying to think of a way to get out of this terrifying request.

On the appointed day I wrote a note to John saying, I was *really* sorry but I had laryngitis and wouldn't be able to give the seminar, and had my friend, Wendy, deliver it. I went home for Christmas the next day, hoping John would have forgotten his request by the time I returned to school. He hadn't, but finding the nerve to make an appointment with him in his office for the first time, I tried to explain that the throat problem was recurring and I wasn't sure when I'd be able to do the seminar. Sitting on the other side of his desk, he just said, "My wife gets laryngitis a lot, too," and let me off the hook. Have I mentioned that John is a kind person?

I *could* express my ideas on paper, though, and liked doing the lit. papers as much as I did my studio art assignments.

Over the years, I've gained some confidence and a *bit* more knowledge. And let's face it, after twenty-five years together, I don't think that John knows absolutely *everything* (although he does know a hell of a lot) and I've been able to speak up for a long time now. Just ask him.

~~~~

Weekends, we walk to the farthest edge of the city, to the park, L'Orangerie, where we have ice cream and watch families play together.

We miss our own and our friends, too.

We go to *vernissages*, listen to string quartets in grand, high-ceilinged palaces and blues concerts at the modern performing arts centre: Ray Charles, B.B. King. We seek out the student quarter where the best and cheapest food is. We walk round and round the wheel-spoked city, over the canals, along the quays. All streets bring us back to the centre of Strasbourg, the Cathedral, where we listen to street musicians and watch artists chalk their magic over the few smooth, uncobbled surfaces of the square.

In time, we notice this about the people of Strasbourg: they're all in love, or rather, in lust. Publicly. They kiss, hold hands, sit on each other's laps in parks, stop cars at busy intersections for long passionate embraces, hold up traffic, and nobody seems to mind!

John and I get caught up in the spirit of things. Privately of course, because we are, after all, Canadian.

~~~~

John wrote this poem for me on my thirty-third birthday:

Renaissance 2
for Jude, on her birthday

sure: its you grinning around the corner of
Maison Des Tanneur's tudor oak beams
a calculated mischief in your eyes like
a gauze rain mocking the cobblestone square

sure: it's you have materialized out of air
in this chipped belching city of bleached stone
have resurfaced out of your denied selves
to inhabit the air like bones rediscovering
a sudden gift of flesh around them again

muscled to them

and as you pivot as suddenly in the air
next to the polished black railing over the quai
almost beguiling this return to living smile

my eye records each transformation as you
gather a body from the sky and rest
your breasts and hips full of time
a Venus moist and solid in the square

. . . so how do we say such things right?
how do we get this down? . . .

I give up and say simply for once
that aside from all the dark corners
we have suffered together you and I
aside from all the deep deaths
we have been lowered into the moist soils of
and aside from our sidelong swipes
at one another in those forced descents
shoved together into those breathless darks

you rise up here before me now
in the thick dust of a Saturday night in Strasbourg
your own full self
sure: I know in the flesh on my own bones
dragged clattering here as witnesses
that somehow this was meant to be
all those cliches about destiny
you know

our slippery love is splayed resilient against time
birth splashed out against itself
you are ripped fiercely out here before me
from the sculpted raw womb of your love
over and over again this birth:
this naked gift of air and
now

September, 1988

The year has been a fantasy realized. We've smiled and laughed a lot and looked around sheepishly, like kids who've gotten away with something. We've gotten away with not just one cookie, but the whole mouth-watering tray! Somehow it feels like that.

Before we leave, I have an exhibition of my paintings in a small gallery where we've been going to see shows and hear music. I have my first review ever in Les Dernieres Nouvelles d' Alsace. John surprises me with it when we meet for coffee at Magmod's. We painstakingly translate the words, brushing almond croissant crumbs away from the print and savouring our afternoon coffee.

> *D'ORIGINE canadienne, Jude Clarke . . . elle vient de passer une année à Strasbourg, y présente avant son départ une sélection d'aquarelles realisées dans les vieux quartiers de la ville. Loin des vues traditionelles, elle voit le passage "comme un système de formes", un peu a la manière de Cezanne. Les tois "s'imbriquent en blocs de couleurs", tandis que "le ciel capricieux crée de beaux jeux de lumière".*
>
> *Privilègiant la sensation, Jude Clarke n'hésite pas à sacrifier le pittoresque aux impératifs de l'organisation et de la recherche d'harmonie dans des oeuvres aerées et lumineuses.*
>
> — M.H.

We are celebrating many things today. John has completed the first draft of his novel and has received word from an agent back in Canada that she's interested in taking a look at it.

~~~~

A couple of days before we're to leave France, we tape a small note to the front door announcing we've got free stuff we want to give away. I'm out when the transaction takes place, but as soon as I return, John tells me, "Our first visitors were the two women from next door and they took most of the furniture!"

I ask, "So did you get a smile?"

"As a matter of fact, I did."

Late October, 1988

I'm standing under a tree, in front of the B&B in Chelsea, our baggage piled around me, waiting for a taxi to take us to the airport. I unzip the black portfolio containing my work and adjust the paintings for the umpteenth time. John is still inside talking to our host. It's a warm sunny day. The sidewalks are clean, the tiny entrance gardens to the row houses immaculate. The row houses lining the other side of the street look elegant, classical even, with their white stucco exteriors and black doors.

I feel wonderfully healthy. Strong. I feel more like my old self than I would ever have thought possible again. I've produced a "show", and have an exhibition set up at home a year from now. There'll be much to do in the preceding year: preparing, finishing up paintings, maybe doing a few new ones, and all the framing. I feel a great sense of accomplishment. *Something happened to me this year. Something wonderful.*

(There was one small incident in Normandy in late August that should have concerned me but I have forgotten or suppressed it. At this moment, I could not be more confident that my good health will continue once I'm back in Canada.)

The air has cooled. The wolf slows her pace. She comes to a stream, dips her head and drinks from the fresh water. Looking around, she sees she has entered a birch grove. Light softly dapples the ground where she stands. Seeing her reflection in the water, she recognizes herself for the first time in a long while. This calms her and she is able to see the wounds she has inflicted upon herself. She licks them and they begin to heal.

John joins me now, under the tree, "Okay. It looks like everything's settled. Here's the cab. Let's go!"

November, 1988

A month after returning from Europe, I drive to the hospital lab for my regular blood and urine tests. A few days later, I see Dr. McAvoy and he tells me that all the test results, except for the urine, show I'm in remission still. The urine test shows I'm spilling two grams of protein. Dr. McAvoy calls Dr. Ballard in Vancouver and he suggests it may just be the amount of protein I'm spilling now, chronically, "It doesn't mean the lupus is active. The kidney disease just does that, but of course, we will keep a close eye on it. You could try 'pulse therapy' and see if that changes the reading."

~~~~

Now I remember being caught in the sun in Normandy. That must have been the trigger. But it could only have been an hour at the most. *Wolf is scoffing, "Just how much time do you think I need?"*

~~~~

It is safe — early morning and overcast — when we start out on our excursion. We are walking from Vernon to Giverny to see Claude Monet's lily ponds. We meander along a grass footpath and look through iron gates into stone courtyards brimming with bright flowers and climbing vines. It's late August and the air is dry and sweet smelling. Along the way, we meet an elderly man, dignified in his black Sunday suit. He takes the time to talk and exuberantly tells us about his town's greatest treasure, the artist Claude Monet. We hear such pride in his voice, as if Monet had created the earth or the sky.

On our return to Vernon in the mid-afternoon, the sky suddenly clears. My black umbrella only draws and intensifies the sun's rays. I panic, the heat is so intense. We have no car. There is no refuge. There is nothing to do but walk. We finally reach the town and stop at a small shop; I stand in the shade under the doorway awning while John goes inside. He comes back out, and hands me a deep-purple plum. I press its cool skin against my burning cheek. When we get back to the hotel I race to the bathroom and throw up.

John leaves. I think he's fed up with me. Later, he says, "I feel like I can't get angry because you always get upset when I do. I end up apologizing to you! That *makes me angry. I'm angry because it's so unfair that we have to think about this disease every day of our lives. I'm angry that we have allowed ourselves to be caught in the sun, like this. Stupidly."*

July 1989

We decide to try "pulse therapy", hoping it will suppress the inflammation — in case that's what it is — in my kidneys. I spend several hours on three alternate days in the hospital receiving massive doses of steroids intravenously.

Nothing changes. Four months later, I'm still spilling two grams of protein.

January, 1990

It's gone. The protein in my urine. There isn't even a trace and won't be for two more years.

Early March, 1990

Just two weeks before my France exhibition opens, I wake one morning to a throbbing back. When I stand up, pain shoots through my entire spine. I wince, and hobble bent over to the bathroom. For the next week, I wait it out — don't call or see my doctor. I'm not going to "up" my steroids. This attack is inexplicable. *Wolf, flexing his muscles.* I haven't had any arthritis since 1986. I walk bent over for almost a week, and then sure enough, just as mysteriously as it began, it goes away, one vertebrae at a time, over a period of another week. One morning I just get up out of bed and walk straight, without a trace of pain.

~~~~

It's opening night at the Topham Brown Art Gallery. Family and friends fill the room. People are asking me about our year away and what inspired me most. I've included several paintings of Kalamalka Lake I did after I returned home, thinking the two different landscapes would make an interesting visual contrast.

One of the lake paintings is entitled *Breakthrough*, which pretty well sums up how I feel about our year in France, both artistically and personally.

From my artist statement for the exhibition *Water: Motion in Place*:

I like to swim long distances in the lake, mostly at dusk. The evening light on the lake is always beautiful, shafts of light reflecting on the water through evening clouds. It's as if I'm swimming in a warm and cool blue pool of light and dark. I exaggerate the blocks of light in my paintings and often make them the central image.

Daytime Kalamalka Lake is a whole other thing. Then, everything dances. Light is fractured and everywhere. The water can be calm and restful, echoing the gentle lines of the surrounding hills, or agitated, waves crashing powerfully against the shoreline. I paint little energies of wind by brushing thin lines across the paper.

October, 1961 (age 6)

"Mom, just ask her. Please, Mom."
"Honey, she doesn't take students this young. And look what your big brother's been doing."
Mom's just discovered that Len's been playing hooky from art lessons for the last three weeks and been hanging around the schoolyard with his friends until five, when ostensibly the art lesson is over, and he can return home safely.
"I would never do that. Mommy, just ask her."
"All right. I will."
A few days later my mother announces, "She says she'll take you! But only on probation. You're going to have to be 'as good as gold.'"
"I will!"
For the next six years, from age six to twelve, Mom drops me off every Wednesday after school at the garage station. I climb the smelly-with-gasoline-and-grease-stairwell and enter Miss Jesse Topham Brown's art studio, where a world of damp clay, wooden drawing boards, pencils, brushes and pots of thick paint awaits me.

September, 1990

As well as painting, I've been teaching art to children on and off for the last ten years. The director of the public art gallery has obtained a grant to develop an art education program, and in the fall I'm offered the part-time position as Education Coordinator. This is to be quite different from the last time I worked at the gallery. The minute I'm offered the position, I tell the director about the lupus and the fatigue I balance every day. No problem. I can work four consecutive five-hour days. Once again, I have a job in the world of art, and now one which involves working with children.

"Your class is here, Jude."

I can hear "the thunder of not-so-tiny hooves" on the stairwell. For the next hour, twenty-eight grade three students exclaim over the huge paintings and "cool" colours. One brave soul somersaults across the expanse of carpeted floor and when I shake my head at him, he exuberantly responds, "This is the neatest place I've ever been in! I'm gonna be an artist when I grow up. My parents have *gotta* see this!"

My favourite moment is a young student seeing the gallery and the art for the first time. There will be an audible intake of breath and a whispered exclamation to the friend beside him or her. There are times when I'm talking about the work and all twenty-eight sets of eyes are transfixed, listening. You could hear a pin drop. Arms shoot straight up when I ask for opinions, and now it's my turn to be awed by the children's naturalness, their unself-conscious eagerness to talk about the art.

~~~~

After a gallery tour with a class, I usually visit the same group of kids at their school and give an art history/hands-on session. I talk about an artist and his or her painting technique and follow with a painting demonstration, the kids huddled around me at a table. A few practically have their noses in the paint. I can relate to this — the delicious look and smell and feel of thick, buttery, tempera paint is irresistible.

"OK, now remember. You need a "galump" of white and a "tutch" of red and blue to make periwinkle."

They roll the new words around in their mouth and say them out loud, giggling at their strangeness. "Galump. Tutch. Periwinkle."

"Hey, can I ask you a question? Are you a *real* artist? Like, have you ever sold a painting?"

"Yes, I have. But you don't have to *sell* your paintings to be an artist. Some of the greatest artists never sell a thing."

My inquisitor looks unconvinced. "Are you gonna be here after lunch? Are we gonna have art all day?"

"No, I've got to get back to the gallery and give another class a tour."

"Oh."

A voice at my elbow pipes up, "I'm going to be an artist, too, when I grow up. I love art."

I turn and give her a smile, "I bet you already are an artist, aren't you?"

"Maybe," she replies shyly.

"OK, everyone. Now it's your turn. Back to your seats and let's get started. Don't forget to be kind to your paintbrushes. Don't scrub and scrunch the hairs into the paper. They'll start screaming if you do." Giggles. "Use a forward and backward motion, gently."

There is a clamour as they rush back to their desks and an explosion of excited voices as they tell each other what colours they're going to make and what they're going to paint.

~~~~

The high-school classes are something quite different.

The boys come in mocking and chucking each other on the shoulder, tripping over their own boat-sized running shoes. The girls seem self-possessed, older than the boys, until someone says something funny and they, too, collapse into collective hilarity. Everyone slumps up against the freshly-painted white walls, bored, spectacularly bored.

I dive in, "So, what do you guys think of the work in this exhibition?"

Dead silence.

"Well, I'll start off then!" I give them some background information on the artist and talk a bit about composition and theme.

One or two heads rise from intense concentration on the gallery carpet. One student actually sits up from his horizontal position on the floor and looks straight at the artwork I'm talking about. I make eye contact with him.

He says gruffly, offhand, "Well, it reminds me of this time I was . . . "

And they're off. Talking and laughing, tentatively at first, then confident. One says, "Well, I think this work sucks!"

"OK. Why do you think that?"

"Because anybody, even Nathan, (jabs Nathan's shoulder) could do it better." Big laughs around the room.

"OK, so now you've got to look at specific things — composition, technique, colour, and decide if there's something there that makes you think it's not good art. Does anyone else have a different reaction to the work?"

"Yeah! It's radical. It rocks!"

"So what is it, specifically, about the work that makes you think that?"

"That dull-blue shape beside the orange one makes the orange look like it's burning. Like fire."

"Good. You've just given the class and me something specific to think about. You don't have to *like* a work of art, but it's a good thing to be able to explain why you do or don't. The next exhibition is an 'installation', an artist's totally different approach to interpreting the world around her. Thanks everybody and I'll see you next month."

~~~~

Aside from walking and swimming, I've been able to play tennis for periods of time over the years. The summer before we went to France, John and I got addicted to the sport. We'd play twice a day: head out to the tennis court with the most shade early in the morning and then again after supper to a different court with just as much shade. I had to work up to it, but eventually my stamina was good.

Dr. McMann, in Regina, had said, "No, not a very good idea for you," when I asked him about cross-country skiing. But he was looking at a skinny, pain-racked, twenty-one-year-old girl at the time. Now, ten years later, I am something quite different. I have no arthritis, no pain of any kind.

~~~~

So we take up cross-country skiing. At the beginning, we go to the golf course for short, flat runs, but eventually drive up Silver Star Mountain. On the mountain, we swoosh along trails under towering pine trees, branches swaying high above our heads. Some days, the branches are draped in heavy wings of snow and darken the trail: other days, delicately laced with hoarfrost, causing light to dance in dappled patterns across the snow in front of us.

A balaclava is perfect for the sunny days — sun reflected off snow can be very dangerous — but it's not comfortable. I immediately feel sweaty from the heat I'm generating under the wool face cap. On overcast or snowy days, I stuff the balaclava, my scarf, sunglasses and even my gloves into my pack and feel sharp pinpricks of ice crystals melting on my face. *Fresh air.* I still wear sunscreen.

Winter, 1991

Mom, Sharon, Franny, John and I and our dog Georgia are out for a short ski run at the local golf course. I'm going along at my usual slow pace. Everyone else is quite far ahead, gliding smoothly on waxed skis. Someone notices I've dropped behind; everyone stops and waits for me to catch up.

The second I reach them — before I can catch my breath — they all push off, and soon I've fallen behind again. A few more minutes and they all look back and come to a standstill. Same scenario. I reach them, puffing, and they all push off. The third time this happens, John blocks my way and says, "Just let them go on ahead. We'll wait here until you're rested. Christ! Has anybody here ever heard the words *lupus* or *chronic fatigue?* Even our families don't get it."

I mutter, "Well, screw them. They're just a bunch of idiots, anyway."

~~~~

Mainly though, after our year in France, our sport becomes walking. We walk various routes, a few days a week. It's simple, requires no equipment and can be adjusted to fit an ever-changing level of energy.

August 1992, Banff, Alberta

I stumble out of the tent in the morning. My eyes feel funny. I head for the women's washroom, look in the mirror. My eyelids are swollen. My eyes are slits. I race back to the tent. *Wolf is at my heels.*

"Look! I must be flaring."

I grab my red pillbox and take out all the prednisone I have for the whole week. Twelve pills, 5 mg each. That's 60 mg in total. It's enough to get me started. I swallow them with milk from the cooler. We take the time to have breakfast in a cafe. We talk calmly, quietly. We are miles away from Vernon. If we don't stop, we can be there by three in the afternoon — in plenty of time to see my doctor.

~~~~

I haven't had a kidney flare in seven years and the fall before had spoken to my nephrologist about reducing the amount of azathioprine, an immunosuppressive I'm taking. I know long-term use increases the risk of cancer. He had agreed and I've been reducing it slowly. I'm tested every month to make sure everything is OK. For six months everything is and then I become cavalier. I don't get tested for three months.

In August, after a tense drive from Banff to Vernon, we get the bad news. A large amount of protein is showing in my urine. My serum creatinine is way up. I've lost more kidney function. Quite a bit, this time. *Never let your guard down. Wildfire can flare at any time.*

I begin steroid treatment and increase the azathioprine to its former dosage. This is to be my worst experience ever with prednisone. Soon, I'm winding up and up into another dimension. I'm flying. My mind is humming, my heart speeding. I'm talking all the time. I can't rest. I can't sleep. My body is vibrating. *John, hold me tight, hold me tight. Hold me still.*

Day and night. Night and day. There is no distinction. I sleep in bits and pieces. Endless time to fill. Waiting for the drugs to work. Waiting to get better. Hungry all the time. Craving sweets. Eating, eating, eating. First, I lose weight, then begin to gain rapidly. My face is swollen, and my eyes are slits between puffy lids — from the prednisone now, not the kidney disease. My neck, breasts and stomach are as swollen as my face. I have what they call a "widow's hump" (who thought that one up?) on my back, at the base of my neck. I stop menstruating. A light brown mustache begins to grow over my upper lip. My hair starts falling out, uniformly at least, not in clumps. It covers my pillow in the mornings. Every time I brush my hair, soft brown strands float to the bottom of the sink bowl and onto the floor. I'm afraid I'll look in the mirror one day and be bald.

Sharon drops by regularly with our young nieces, Sarah and Alison. Their company comforts me, keeps me going.

Mid-October, 1992

"Of course you can't, honey. Nobody expects you to."

Mom and I are standing in my studio looking out at the side garden. We can see five mounds of freshly-heaved earth. She has just dug five twelve-inch-deep holes for me. I'd sprinkled the bottoms with bone meal and placed twelve, red Darwin tulip bulbs in each hole. I'd ordered them especially from Cruickshanks, in Ontario.

"Of course not. Because I'm the sick one, aren't I? *The sick one.*" My hands are clenched at my sides. My whole body is tense. I want to kick the wall or pick up my treasured paints and throw them across the room. I am thirty-seven. Mom is seventy. At the age I am now, she was the mother of four children. Today, my seventy-year-old mother is digging my garden for me.

~~~~

I slam my fist into the bed. "I *hate* this disease. It's the *worst* possible disease for a person like me to have. *Nobody* knows what it's like. *You* don't know what its like. It just me and this fucking disease when it comes right down to it. I'm just so fucking pissed off. I can't even walk across the street to say "hi" to the neighbours when the sun's out. *You know.* It's like danger everywhere. Can you imagine what it feels like to be *so* afraid of the sun? And then, as if that's not enough, oh, ya, *right!* How about my kidneys? How are they doing these days? Any more deterioration? How much closer am I to end-stage kidney failure? Every three months, it's time to do my lab tests again. They stick that needle in and take out four vials of blood and I pee a urine sample in the bathroom and stare at it trying to decide if the pee's the right colour. Is it cloudy or clear? Christ! Sarah and Alison can't visit me on their way home from school because I'm sleeping. My day is *six fucking hours long*. Then I collapse. Sleep the sleep of the dead. And then it takes an hour to come to. To feel halfway all right. I *hate* that hour before supper. I always feel like shit. I just have to give and give and give to this disease. No matter what I give up or how careful I am, it's *never enough*. I'm always trying so hard. I'm *sick* of trying so hard."

Late October, 1992

I walk halfway to the college with John some mornings, until the prednisone thins my skin to the point that the rims of my running shoes are too much pressure and the entire tops of both feet turn blue, swollen and bruised.

I go to my once-weekly appointment with Dr. McAvoy and on this day, after the usual examination and discussion about my lab results, I casually say, "Oh there's one more thing John made me promise to show you." I take off one shoe and a sock. It is the only time I've ever seen Dr. McAvoy visibly alarmed. He won't let me go home. I phone John and meet him at the hospital; x-rays are taken and a rheumatologist examines me. I keep explaining, "It's just from the walking. We don't have to worry. I've stopped walking." I'm right. It is just from the walking. The whole thing is surreal.

Dr. McAvoy greets me when I come through his office door a few days later with, "You've got to tell me these things, you know." There is real reproach in his voice "You scared me. I had no idea you were such a 'walker'." Stern look.

"Walking is one of the things that keeps me sane during a flare. But I will tell you these things from now on."

So now I can't walk.

I organize the house, sort through hundreds of photographs I've never put in albums, colour-coordinate the clothes in my closet. *Really.* I bake. I try to paint, but I can't. I can't concentrate. I discover that music, in the middle of the night, calms my metabolism. I move from our bedroom to the living-room couch and place the headphones over my ears. I crank up the volume until it drowns out the chaos in my head. First, I always listen to side two of the second cassette of Van Morrison's "a night in san francisco". It's a medley of Van's songs interspersed with some of Sam Cooke's lyrics. Van sings about being alone in the night and what Paradise is like. He describes space in terms of the night. *I know what he means.* Then, he's singing the words to "Darling, you send me" but wait . . . no, that's Brian Kennedy's angel voice. Now Van's back chanting the words to "No Guru No method No teacher". *I agree, Mr. Morrison. It works for me.*

Now quick! Push the Stop button. "Shakin' all Over" is next and I'm already shaking enough from the prednisone. "Gloria" is after that. It's a rock and roll song, and this just isn't a rock and roll kind of night. Rewind, press play again.

Van Morrison knows. He knows how to say it, too. Just listen to "Sometimes We Cry" on *The Healing Game.*

December, 1992

By Christmas, the kidney flare is under control and I begin reducing the prednisone, large amounts at first and then increasingly smaller amounts. Almost immediately, I begin to sleep and sleep and sleep. I am as bone tired now as I was wound up a few weeks ago. I am determined to return to work.

I return in January. Too soon. I tell John, "I have to. I just have to." I think I might disappear if I leave the working world, the outside world where I feel included, where I'm finally at ease with my disease. I don't ever again want to be that withdrawn, hesitant person I remember so well from long ago. I don't trust myself not to turn back into her. I get through each day, then collapse from fatigue when I get home. I will not give up. I will not let myself give up. It would be so easy (and maybe even smart) to resign. Stay home. Paint, garden, swim. Have a slower life. But that isn't an option in my head. I'm not ready. I still want the job and I still think I need the job — that it defines me, in a way.

~~~~

My sister Franny drops by the house almost every day after work. She sits quietly across from me. She never gives advice. She listens. When she does say something, I listen to her like I've always listened to her, with the complete and utter devotion of a younger sister.

Spring, 1971 (age 16)

Mom shrieks, "Look! It's Franny! It's our wandering gypsy home at last." I run to the window and see my sister coming across the lawn, grinning, laden down with a backpack and a duffel bag. A tarnished copper pot hangs from her waist. Her strawberry-blonde hair flows down her back. Franny has arrived home out of the blue. We all thought she was still in Morocco. She plops her bags down on the living-room carpet and starts pulling out treasures. I'm sitting on the floor beside her, enthralled. I can't take my eyes off her. She hands me a long white and blue cotton robe. "And this is for you, Jude. It's called a *jellaba* and they wear them in Morocco. And these are Mauritania beads." Hundreds of brightly-patterned, opaque glass beads spill onto the floor.
I am sitting in a field of jewel-flowers.
Franny says, "Aren't they trippy? I'm going to make necklaces out of them and sell them around town."
They are the most beautiful things I have ever seen.

~~~~

I've been back at work for six weeks when I drive to her house one evening. "I don't know what's wrong with me. I'm better now. My kidneys are fine. I'm almost back to my usual low maintenance dose of prednisone. I should be happy and relieved I'm through this. But I'm crying all the time and I can't seem to feel anything but depressed. I don't know what's wrong with me."

My sister is the one who uncovers the information that steroids can induce depression. I didn't know this before this flare. I had always assumed that the depression I experienced after a flare was just because I had been so sick for so long. And also, because the prednisone had caused such horrible, visible side effects. And because I knew it would be months and months before I felt well and strong again.

Or, that it was just me.

Why hadn't I been told? I talk to my doctor and ask to be referred to a good psychologist. I don't even consider more drugs to offset the depression. I've swallowed enough pills. I ask to be referred to Jennifer Thompson, who is the daughter of the doctor who delivered me (only in a small town). We have the kind of connection I had hoped for. We laugh at the same kinds of things. She feels a bit like family since her father delivered my brothers and sister, too. She's "old Vernon". I talk about my fears when I was first diagnosed with lupus, my ongoing anxieties, how my father's illness affected me as a child and my relationship with my mother.

~~~~

When I was small, Mom and I were the best of buddies. Because I was the youngest child, we spent a lot of time together, just she and I, before I started school — and even after. I idolized her with the innocence of a child. She wasn't like the other moms I knew; she was *fun*! I thought I would grow up to be just like her — beautiful, capable of doing anything. Most of all, I would be a mom just like her.

Then I became ill. Fatigue and arthritis pain sapped more and more of my energy. I still thought I could be just like Mom; it would just take more of an effort. But I felt I was nothing like her. People were drawn to her. We couldn't walk down the main street of town together without stopping ten times to chat to someone. When I was little, I noticed everyone smiled and laughed more when she was around. When I was older, and sick, trying to just get through a day, she came to represent something I could never be.

After I was diagnosed with lupus, I became withdrawn with people other than my closest friends. I became someone quite opposite to that seventeen-year-old girl who "knew her life was about to begin". Though at that age I had been shy meeting new people, *painfully* shy with people I especially admired or had a "crush" on, I was an extrovert with my friends, always ready for fun and adventure, always finding lots to laugh about. Now I had become so unsure of myself, of so many things.

Wolf had my body. But it felt as if he wouldn't be satisfied until he had everything. He wanted my soul, too.

146

My introspection revolved around what a huge disappointment I must be to everyone. Most of all, what a huge disappointment I was to myself. I criticized myself for having a disease. I overcompensated. One day, I would go like mad, get lots of things done, throw a party, will myself to be the person I wanted to be. The next day, I'd collapse, spend the day in bed, exhausted and tense because I was in bed instead of carrying on like a "normal" person. I set up impossible expectations. I couldn't win. And I couldn't see that Wolf was only half my problem. *I* was the other half. Giving myself no room to breathe. Showing myself no mercy.

This began to change when I turned thirty, and more so when John and I went to France. We were far from home and seeing so many new things and feeling such excitement and freedom. I said that Wolf stayed behind in Canada that year but John says that I left part of myself back home, too. My self-critical self. My worried self. I started to see myself as a painter there. I was a painter who happened to have a disease. I felt myself coming back as if through a long, grey, airless tunnel, into the light.

I began to see that my nature was not only to despair and to analyze and to worry. What did I think was getting me through this chronic illness? It wasn't just the love I felt from John or my family and friends. It was something in me. I began to see that it was also my nature to feel a simple thrill when I discovered the green tips of crocus shoots poking through the earth in the spring. To laugh a lot. To enjoy the children in my life with a natural ease. To go to France without a moment's hesitation. To be happy. It seemed, now, that these instincts were just as strong — perhaps even stronger — than the ones that made me so self-critical.

I wasn't a failure. I was just living a different story. One that demanded different things. It's true that my mother is one of those rare individuals born with a naturally happy outlook. She worries, but she doesn't analyze everything. She has her own vulnerabilities, her own sorrows, but she lives on a level that sees and feels hope naturally above despair. But Mom is also much more. As I found out in time, her life has never been as simple as I thought it was, and she herself, never that free.

~~~~

My mother and father were married in the garden of her childhood home in Whitby, Ontario, in 1947. They had met just a year before in Vernon, soon after my mother had arrived to fill a nursing position, newly graduated from the University of Toronto. My father had been working for his father as a pharmacist, playing tennis, and according to my mother, "dating just about every girl in town!"

They drove back out west in a brand new Dodge Club Coupe my grandfather had loaned them the money to buy, began a life together and eventually had four children within eight years. Boy. Girl. Boy. Girl. First Len, Franny, Joe, and then me, the youngest. My mother tells me that right after they were married, my father told her that he wanted her to go back to visit her family whenever she felt the need to see them. She took him up on it and every couple of years she'd take two of us kids, ("*never* more than *two* at a time!") back east to meet our cousins (in time these numbered twenty-four).

Those train trips across Canada, beginning with the slow, curling ascent into the Rocky Mountains and the similarly-paced descent, were the biggest and most exciting adventures of my childhood. Reaching the prairies, the train would pick up speed, whistling through miles and miles of wheat fields, heralding our arrival at each township with several long, low hoots of the horn. At last, we would enter the great forests of Ontario, make a final, wide curve around Lake Superior and soon reach our destination — the city of Toronto.

~~~~

My father started showing signs of manic depression when he was in his mid-forties. My mother was in her late thirties, three thousand miles away from her parents, sister and four brothers. She had left a boisterous, close family in Ontario to live one street up from my father's family in Vernon. They weren't boisterous and though they were unfailingly loyal to one another, they didn't particularly seem to like, or for that matter, even to *dislike* each other.

It wasn't until after my father died that my mother began to talk more freely about his illness and how it affected *her.*

Just recently, Mom and I had a long conversation about this. I wanted to know more about her and Dad's life together, especially when he was ill. She couldn't have guessed why I needed her to talk, but I knew. I had a feeling this information would reveal a lot about how I see and cope with illness myself. Mom was seventy-eight years old at the time we had this conversation and I was forty-four.

She and I were sitting in armchairs in the living room of my childhood home. I didn't know if I could draw her out in the way that I wanted to, but we'd been sharing some laughs and were both relaxed. I sensed this was the right time. I took the direct approach and — lo and behold — it worked.

~~~~

Setting my coffee mug on the mahogany side table, I slump back into my armchair. "How did you do it Mom? How did you cope with Dad's illness?"

She replies simply and easily, "I was just so happy. I loved your father and I loved you kids."

She pauses, then looks right at me, her expression serious now. "I haven't had a life like yours, Jude. It seemed we just kept having babies. You were all surprises and you were all wanted. I wasn't the type of person who could have done two things at once: raise a family and work as a nurse, too. I wanted to be home with you. And I look at all of you now and see how close you are and how much you trust one another and I know your father and

I provided that for you, the environment that made it possible to build those relationships. I grew up in a family like that, and your father more than anything wanted that for our own family. I'm so proud of all of you. You four kids are my paintings. *Philippe!* Get off the chair!"

Philippe, the cat from Quebec, slowly backs down the chair, snagging the cotton material as he descends, reaches the carpet, retracts his claws and walks away, aloof and disdainful; Finnegan yips from the back hall. She's there to dry off and figures it's time to be let in. She races towards the den to find the cat as soon as I open the door.

Back in my chair, not wanting to lose the moment, I press on: "But, day to day, how did you cope? Wasn't it hard?"

Mom's face tightens a little. "Yes, it was hard seeing your Dad so defeated and critical of himself. He worried about all kinds of things. He was right there with me, always calm and steady in the big crises in our lives, but it was the little things I couldn't have cared less about that bothered him. And he'd get mad. Your father saw injustice and he saw stupidity and it bothered the hell out of him. Pomposity amused him but arrogance bothered him."

Shifting in her chair, her brow furrows and she says, "You know your father should never have been in business. Having the responsibility of owning and managing a store. Dealing with the public and a staff day to day. That's a hard job. Your dad had a strict code of behaviour and ethics that he lived by and he just *hoped* that other people — staff and customers — would follow the same code. But people disappointed him. He'd come home and talk to me about the things people said and did. He took everything to heart. Running the store was so hard on him."

Kicking off my shoes, I blurt out something I have often thought. "Dad should have been a historian. He would have loved the quiet of that." I have a memory of piles of Dad's thick, hardcover history books with important titles lying on coffee tables around our house, comingling with his favourite Westerns, Louis Lamour paperbacks.

Now I straighten up in my chair and look beyond Mom to the bookcase behind her chair. There's the set by Winston Churchill: *The Hinge of Fate*, *The Grand Alliance*, *The Gathering Storm*, and *Their Finest Hour*. I can see two "Merck Manuals". I know without checking they're new, updated books — Dad had thrown the old one out years ago, the day we had all first read about lupus in it. I'm looking for a certain book, a certain colour and size. *Bingo! There it is. Roget's Thesaurus.* Once in a while, throughout my childhood, I'd be looking for something new to read and pull this book out. I thought it was a book about a boy and his dinosaur. The first couple of times I'd done this, I had forgotten what it really was. After that, I think I just hoped each time that somehow, magically, it had transformed into a book about a dinosaur.

Today, I feel comforted by its discovery. The book is exactly as it was, after all these years. Its presence seems almost holy.

I get up and go over to the fireplace. Mom had the real one fitted with a gas insert after Dad died so she wouldn't have to worry about chopping wood and bringing it up from the basement. Leaning over, I turn the knob; flames poof and I curl up on the floor next to the fire, welcoming the instant warmth on my back.

Mom squints and gently rubs her eyes. "My eyes are really bothering me today. Your grandmother had dry eyes, too."

I make a sound of sympathy. She flaps her hand at me. "They're fine." She settles back into her chair, putting her feet up on the hassock in front of her. I can tell she's enjoying our conversation. She hasn't told this story very often.

"It was always just assumed your Dad would inherit the drugstore and his older brother the big family home. Your father's brother was an army man. Big and confident. Your Dad wasn't accepted into the army because his eyesight was so bad. He was a sensitive boy living in a distant, disapproving and pretty humourless family. I remember arriving ahead of your dad in Whitby to help Mom get ready for our wedding. Mom asked me what your dad was like and what his family was like. I said, "They're a fine family but they don't seem to have much fun together." Your Auntie Evelyn (my father's only sister) put it another way. She said, "We all lived in the same house but were emotionally separate, almost as if we lived in different compartments.""

I remember all the when-I-was-young stories told to us by my mother about her family. As teenagers, we'd roll our eyes — here she goes, life on the farm — and groan audibly when a story would be prefaced with, "When I was in public health . . . " In those days we had trouble picturing her as anything but "Mom". Dad would never say much of anything about his own family. Later, when I was older, and would occasionally press him for specifics, he'd invariably say, "I can't really think of anything," then add, with a droll look on his face, "But your mother has all kinds of exciting stories about life on the farm!"

We hear a crash in the den. Philippe streaks into the room and behind Mom's chair. Finnegan arrives seconds later. She comes to an abrupt stop. She looks like a cartoon character — "I tawt I taw a puddytat" — as she looks frantically around. Philippe sticks a paw out from behind the chair, taunting her, and they're off again, down the hallway to one of the bedrooms.

"I bet they've knocked over a plant in the den," Mom says in exasperation. Neither of us gets up to see.

"Your father found his niche in tennis." Mom gets a faraway look. "He was beautiful to watch: agile, accurate and graceful. He was so slight and would play so hard, he'd lose ten pounds over a tournament weekend. He won the men's singles championship for the valley one year and ten years later won it again."

Dad's tennis trophies still line a shelf in the cabin kitchen. He wouldn't have put them on display. Mom would have done that. The summer after Dad died, Mom set up the Reid Clarke Memorial trophy for the juniors competition at the Kalamalka Lake Country Club. Dad taught us all how to play tennis out there, and though

154

none of us ever became the champion he was, we're all pretty good; we've inherited his hand/eye coordination.

Her face lights up: "Your Dad and I had a lot of fun together. He had the greatest wit. He could be so irreverent. I loved that about him. I knew my life would never be dull with him."

Suddenly, her voice rising in exasperation, "He also drove me nuts. He was so finicky, so careful. He'd take forever to make a decision about the smallest thing. I just wanted to do it. Right then! I was as impulsive as he was cautious."

Her voice becomes fierce: "And sometimes it was just a pain trying to build him up all the time. I enjoyed a good fight. He'd think it was the end of the world and fold on me. That really made me mad. I wanted him to yell back."

John always yells back.

Mom adds wryly, "I suppose *I* drove *him* nuts, too."

I say quickly, "Yeah, the only way we knew you guys were working something out was when you'd banish us all from the dinner table. The door would shut. There was never any yelling — just an air of cool politeness towards each other when you came out. That didn't prepare me at all for the real world."

As soon as I say this, I know she isn't going to let it slip by. Mom's too feisty for that. She opens her eyes wide and says dryly, "I suppose it would have been better for us to yell a lot. Make life miserable for you?"

Now we're getting somewhere. My skin is tingling. I say evenly, innocuously, "No, but I wouldn't have had the impression that you were handling everything so perfectly."

Lifting her chin a little, she says, "I wanted to protect you. I didn't want our problems to be yours."

But they were, Mom. We knew Dad was sick.

Don't you see, it taught me that illness should be handled by oneself. You raised the bar so high in your resolute determination to give us a good life, to protect us from your pain, that when I became ill, there was only one acceptable way in my head to cope with it: to carry on as if nothing was wrong. I tried that for eight years. But I wasn't you. When I couldn't keep up the façade any longer, I didn't just feel like a failure. I knew I was a failure.

I say intensely, "But it wasn't good that you kept up that front."

Mom looks at me and admits quietly, "I know, but it was the only way I knew how. At the time, there was still a big stigma attached to mental illness. You didn't talk about it. I didn't want to talk about it. It was pride, too. And wanting to protect our privacy."

Now my heart is aching and I'm confused. At this moment, I'm not sure who I feel most badly for — my mother or myself.

I say, "I admired you so much, Mom. I still do."

Self-mocking, doing her, "keep it coming" gesture with her hands, her face relaxes and she says, "I felt the same way about *my* mother, Jude. She was always so calm and patient and capable. I wanted those qualities, too, but I just didn't have them. Your Aunt Mary got them all, damn it!"

Laughing, she runs a hand through her hair. My mother had thick, auburn hair until her mid-twenties when it began to turn grey. My earliest memories of her are of a slim, vibrant woman with lustrous, silver hair.

~~~~

I remember sitting on the end of her bed one night when I was a child, watching her dress for a party. She pulled a long, simply-cut green dress over her slip, picked up a pair of long white gloves off the dresser and drew them over her arms. I remember the elegance of that gesture. She smoothed her hair, drew a pink lipstick over her lips and twirled round for my benefit.

"Mommy, you're beautiful!"

"And you, my Darling, are my 'Best Booster'!"

~~~~

Mom has arthritis now, but when asked about it, she tosses the pain off cavalierly, explaining, "I'm tight in the morning but it works itself out in an hour or so. My back's sore the day after I play golf but then I'm fine." A couple of years ago, Mom began experiencing severe pain down one leg. Her doctor arranged an appointment with a back surgeon. Mom announced, "I've got two months to cure myself. I'm *not* going to have surgery." And by God, she did it. She went on daily walks believing that physical activity would cure the problem. Personally, I think she *willed* the problem away. She never did keep that appointment. It wasn't necessary.

John always tells Mom, with a devilish look in his eye, "Betty, you're going to be standing over my grave saying, 'He should have looked after himself, poor old soul. He never did do anything by halves.' We all laugh and then laugh even harder because we're all thinking it's not entirely out of the realm of possibility.

I look at her hands now, clasped around her coffee mug. The finger joints are swollen, the flesh pulled tight over the knuckles. I say gently, "What was the first sign of Dad's illness?"

Tugging first one cuff of her sweater sleeve and then the other over each wrist, she thinks for a minute. "I do remember the first time, clearly, that I thought something was wrong. Your father and I had been next door having a drink with a few of the neighbours. We'd forgotten to take something over — I forget what — and came back to the house to get it. I remember standing in the kitchen with him and suddenly being aware that he was abnormally agitated, irritated about something someone had said at the party. Slowly, insidiously really, these incidents became more and more frequent. By the time he was in his late forties, he went into his first deep depression and had to take time off from the store. He tortured himself about that, worried about our finances, worried about the future, felt inadequate. Nothing I could say or do seemed to reassure him or calm his fears."

Her face becomes pensive. "I remember one evening we got a babysitter and went out to the cabin to have some time to ourselves. We were standing on the shore. I reached down and picked up a few pebbles and tossed them one by one into the water. I said, "See Reid. See the circles moving outwards from where the pebbles drop. How natural and peaceful that is. Can you think of yourself as one of those circles, reaching out, letting the pain you feel move outwards, naturally, instead of trying to hold it all inside."

"That was a beautiful thing to tell him, Mom."

She reaches up with one hand and massages her neck. *Her neck must be bothering her today, too.* "It just felt right to try and look at it that way. He was finally diagnosed with manic depression and was ill off and on for the next twelve years. Then, his doctor put him on lithium, and as you know he never experienced another manic-depressive cycle again. He had ten level "well" years. That was a gift, you know, for both of us."

"And for us kids, too."

The phone rings. Mom picks it up from the table beside her. "Hello? Yes dear, come on up. Jude's here, too. We're having coffee."

"Franny," Mom says as she places the receiver back in its cradle. "She'll be up in a bit."

Mom stands and goes over to the window. *She's still so fit. She's only just stopped cross-country skiing. Why didn't I get some of those indefatigable McQuay genes?* Mom's brother, Norman, and his wife, Jean, are coming to visit in February. Uncle Norm will be hitting the downhill ski slopes with Aunt Mary. *Uncle Norm is eighty years old for God's sake. He just bought a brand new set of skis and boots. Aunt Mary is seventy-four.*

Mom muses, "I'm going to have to get someone up to take a limb off the catalpa. It looks like it could break any minute."

Back in her chair, she continues: "You know your grandfather trained at the Mayo Clinic. He got his first position as a diagnostician and a surgeon at a hospital in Portage La Prairie, in Manitoba. He always had had migraines and eventually they made it impossible for him to do surgery. He was offered a position as a diagnostician in Toronto, so Mom and he moved the family to Ontario. That's when Dad bought the farm in Whitby."

I'm sitting cross-legged, chin in my hands, elbows supported by my knees, listening intently.

"Dad hired men to work and run the farm and he commuted to the city every day. Mom was home running the household and raising us kids. Fourteen people sat down at our dinner table every night: the nine of us, two elderly relatives, the woman who'd been hired to help Mom and the two men who lived and worked on the farm."

Phillipe steals into the room and jumps onto her lap. *I wonder where Finnegan is?*

Stroking the cat's back, Mom says quietly, "I was just eighteen when my brother Francis died from tetanus poisoning. He was only twenty-three. He'd been working in a dairy in Oshawa and had somehow cut himself. Your Uncle Norm says that at that time, no one was aware yet that there is a significantly higher risk for tetanus poisoning with any work involving animals. Francis started feeling sick and the man he was working for sent him home, to Whitby. The night before he died, all of us kids were in his room having a gay old time, like we always did. The next morning we were woken by the sound of Francis having a seizure . . . "

My body is rigid. Mom is far away, reliving that moment, her face vulnerable.

"I can still hear it. Dad called the neurosurgeon in Toronto to come. The doctor was taking too long, so Dad called the neurosurgeon at the psychiatric hospital in Whitby. I remember both doctors arriving at the same time, but it was too late. Francis died.

Dad didn't find out it was tetanus until the autopsy was performed. I don't think he ever got over the fact that he couldn't save his own son. A couple of years later, he gave up practising medicine altogether. He retired at fifty-four and strangely enough, so did your own father. Fifty-four. All of that must have prepared and helped me cope with your father's illness."

I'm quiet, thinking of how terrible this must have been. Franny is named for Mom's brother.

Now, something occurs to me. "You told your parents about Dad's illness, didn't you?"

"No, I never did."

"But Mom!"

"What could they do? They were so far away, they'd just have worried."

"But Mom."

I can't take in the enormity of what she's just told me. And then I remember having a conversation with Aunt Mary in our kitchen a few days after Dad died. She and

Uncle Norm had flown right out from Ontario to be with Mom. I said something about Dad's manic depression. Aunt Mary looked a little blank. "Has Mom never talked to you about Dad's illness?"

"Not really."

I suddenly envision my mother, three thousand miles away from her family with a sick husband and four children, carrying on, keeping life as normal as possible for all of us. She couldn't bring herself to tell her own family — not even her sister — so how could she let her children who she only wanted to protect know or see that she was struggling. I can't ask my mother another question. I am too overwhelmed with grief for her to continue.

Mom wants to change the conversation, anyway. She deftly takes the focus off herself, and turns it on me. "*You* cope so well, yourself, honey."

I draw my legs up and wrap my arms around my knees, hands interlaced. "Oh, for so long I didn't think that. I constantly measured myself against you. You had four children and managed to keep up that indomitable spirit of yours, in spite of Dad's illness. You were a hard act to follow."

"But you know that we were struggling too, and scared."

"*Now* I do."

Mom ignores this but says, "And don't forget, Jude, it was your father who was sick. I was healthy. I wouldn't and couldn't have gone ahead and had four babies if I'd been the one with the health concerns."

Feeling my sense of humour break through, I announce in an "up on my soapbox kind of voice", "Which is just another reason why men should be able to get pregnant. John could have had our babies."

Mom hoots. "Hah! Wouldn't that be something?"

But now I want to say something serious. My hands tighten their clasp. "During the last flare, I felt the burden of fear being lifted from me. I allowed it to be lifted. I had grown so used to living with my fears that they had become a part of me. So I consciously had to decide to let them go. Dad's illness, the kind of kid I was. I thought he was dying and we couldn't do anything about it. And every time I had a headache, I thought maybe this would be the one that would kill me. I thought your brother Francis had died from a headache. I must have got the story of his dying mixed up with something you'd said about grandpa having migraines."

My voice breaks. "Then I was diagnosed with lupus. I just got more and more tense and I was so scared every time I went to the doctor. What will I be told today? What terrible fear will be confirmed today? I couldn't catch my breath. I felt like I was drowning. I couldn't get through the dark. It was my childhood nightmare. *Caught in tangled ropes forever.* And nobody could fix it."

Mom's face is crestfallen. "Your father and I wanted so badly to fix it. We were so scared, too."

My mind flashes back to a day about a year before I was diagnosed. I was in Vernon, John in Toronto. I'd just come back to my parent's home from a doctor's appointment. For the last month, my doctor had had me trying out increasingly higher doses of

163

aspirin for the arthritis pain. I was supposed to keep taking more and more pills until my ears started to ring, which would mean I'd reached my limit and the aspirin was actually poisoning me. I think I got up to about seventeen pills a day and it hadn't even touched the pain. This day, the doctor had prescribed something new for me to try, a drug called prednisone.

I find Mom downstairs doing laundry. Waving the prescription order in the air, I say, "I'm going to be taking pills for the rest of my life." It comes out hard. Accusingly. I'm daring her to disagree with me. Wanting her to disagree with me. She does disagree, but in the wrong tone of voice,

"Don't be ridiculous. That's a ridiculous thing to say."

I thought then that Mom was angry with me, even that she was dismissing my pain and whatever it was that was happening inside my body.

Of course it wasn't anger. It was fear.

Now, I call out, "Finnegan! Phillipe's in here . . . " She appears through the kitchen doorway, blinking groggily, face hair scrunched up in that telltale way. She's been sleeping. She glances at Phillipe and lies down, flat out, facing me. I rub her head and she closes her eyes.

"But John and I were already together."

Mom laughs. "I remember that night at the cabin when you told me your plans. I remember thinking, I don't have a hope of talking this child out of going to Toronto to be with this man. I must say, even though I was worried, I was in awe of your sureness."

"Says she who introduced her beloved husband to her parents three days before she was to be married."

Mom grins sheepishly.

"Mom, from the beginning, John's love made me feel safe. Just hearing his voice, just being with him could ease my fears. It's still that way. He just has to brush his hand across my cheek. It calms me. I can feel his love in that touch. I know."

Mom's eyes are welling.

My own fill. "My love for him is the one thing the lupus hasn't been able to touch. It carries me through my darkest nights. Disease is helpless up against it. The great thing is that I've always known this, all along the way. It's given me a kind of power. Even on the darkest nights, I can feel that power."

There's a light knock at the front door and the sound of the door opening. Mom says, "Here's Franny." Louder, "Come on in, dear."

I stand up and give my whole body a shake. "Phew! Thank God. One more minute and we'd have been two puddles on the floor. Not something we'd want anyone to see. Right, Mom?"

Smiling, "Right, Jude."

~~~~

My maternal grandfather, a physician, retired at the age of fifty-four. My mother thinks he never got over the fact that he couldn't save his own son, who died at the age of twenty-three from tetanus poisoning. My father, a pharmacist, retired at the age of fifty-four, too. He suffered the debilitating cycles of manic depression for over ten years before they were finally leveled out with lithium. He experienced his last depression in the winter of 1976. A year later, on Valentine's Day, 1977, I began experiencing severe chest pain. The next day I was admitted to hospital and diagnosed with pericarditis, an inflammation of the heart lining. A few days later, I was told I had a disease named Systemic Lupus Erythematosus, that it had no known cure and that I would have it for the rest of my life. Eight years after that, on Valentine's Day, my father had bypass surgery. He died the next day. My mother lost her best friend when he died.

These are the facts. What they tell me is that there are many ways a heart can be broken.

~~~~

John wrote this poem in the early eighties, when he had known my parents for about six years. The third section is written in my mother's voice:

and who will speak for me?   for my winter?

I stand here at this kitchen sink
wiping its stainless steel walls and fixtures
I can stare at how spotless I keep this white arborite
or how intricate with colour I have fashioned this room

through this window there's our birch in the snow
white on white   so slight   dwarfed by the catalpa
which looms a dark minotaur over the lawn
stretching its stark amber network everywhere
composing shadows shifting on the snow and shrubs
like lace on a maple table drawn by the sun

such a brilliant coloured scene wrapped around me
like a shawl   my wintered home   and me:
the eye which defines it   breathes it into life

breathed my children into life long ago with him

we move about this house now together and alone
the two of us rearrange the lamps vacuum the long
blue rug free of the mindless dog's hair   move
the TV into the bedrom from the den to save on heat
plan trips   have people over   watch the PGA Tour
Saturdays and Sundays: white weekend reveries
of what we'll do all summer out on the loping
memorized course we play   always a surprise
regardless of our devious green memories

thoughts of other seasons divide and fill out this one
that's true   but the season itself is full
the whites so varied and capable of
enlarging each object   of carrying me back to Whitby
in the 30s   to those old Saturday novels and Norman
Rockwell certainies: the preparations for Christmas
the homecomings   then the slowly slowly savoured
withdrawal of all this white into tentative
then blasting greens and yellows: spring
so it's not simply a time to wait   but do
and see   more meditative in its music

the children drop by thick with their lives
so grown up and hesitant in the moves of adults:
one worries about the investment in his house
another is having trouble with her croton

my youngest worries why she gets depressed
my healthiest announces he won't be by for a week

I receive them one by one   am conscious
of their solicitude   a deep irony in me
their lives whirling in such brand new worlds
yet leaning on our old one for definitions
as they pull up on the asphalt in their cars

these many gardens I have tended
so meticulous in my deliberations
under that pendulous sun in my straw hat
or through the window with a coffee in this   winter:
arranging   planning things   waiting for seeds
to break soil

August, 1994

We fly out of Vancouver — destination: Edinburgh —
where we are to spend John's second writing sabbatical.
As the flight progresses, I feel more and more feverish. I
can see red spots appearing on my face and neck in the
ghoulish light of the airplane bathroom. I tell John it's
probably just a twenty-four-hour flu bug. We depart the
plane in London, I with the anxiety that it's something
else — this doesn't feel like just flu — but I don't voice
my worry yet. Our friends, who are loaning us their car
for the year while they're living in our house back in
Canada, pick us up at the airport and we spend the first
night with them at their home in Crowthorne.

In the morning, Malcolm drives us to the Royal Berkshire Hospital in Reading. The emergency waiting room is noisy, flooded with people, and we wait for three hours before I'm finally called into an examining room. By this time, my face and neck are covered in spots. I suspect they're elsewhere on my body, too, judging by how uncomfortable I feel. My muscles feel like jelly. When the doctor enters the examining room, I tell him I have lupus with kidney involvement and hand him my medical file which I've brought with me. I'm immediately admitted and taken to the isolation wing of the hospital in a wheelchair. John walks beside me while the attendant pushes the wheelchair. None of us say a word down corridor after long corridor. It feels like we're being taken to the bowels of the earth. We finally reach the room and a nurse brings in a cot when John asks if it would be possible for him to stay the night.

Another doctor — an internist, I think — questions me for a long time and then tells me he doesn't know what's wrong yet, but because of my medical history he's going to put me on intravenous antiviral medication.

There's no relief. I feel sicker and more feverish as the night wears on and can't sleep or even lie still. Finally, I ask a nurse if I could take a shower. That might help. It does while I'm in the shower but then I hear a commotion outside and the nurse runs in saying, "the shower is leaking through to the lower floor." She sees my face for the first time in the light and says, "Oh. You are going to have a rough night of it."

After a couple more sleepless hours, I ask the nurse if she could fill a towel with ice. I place it on my neck and when the ice numbs the discomfort, I move it to my forehead. This works. I fall asleep.

The next day, many different physicians come and ask specific questions that I assume pertain to their area of expertise. John follows the doctors out into the corridor, and sounding remarkably like Detective Columbo says, "I wonder . . . if I may . . . I would like to ask you . . . I wonder, if my wife, does not have chicken pox?" The doctors would nod indulgently, and say, "It's a bit premature to arrive at that conclusion." Finally, the skin specialist, jovial and pleased, three days after I'm admitted, examines me and announces my condition a textbook case of chicken pox.

~~~~

After a weeklong stay in the hospital, we leave Reading under duress. Just as I'm signing the release forms, a young intern who knows nothing of my case looks at the results of my last serum creatinine test. The reading is significantly higher than it has been all week. The intern, concerned, recommends we stay in Reading. It's a holiday weekend. The doctors who've been treating me have already left the hospital, will be away for three days, and the thought of staying in a hotel worrying about possible kidney failure is too much for either of us. John says, "We have a letter of introduction for Dr. Wheeler in

Edinburgh. We'll drive straight to the hospital for his consultation. It'll be better to do this."

The young intern says, "But you won't be able to just walk in off the street and hope to see him."

I smile reassuringly and say, "Yes, we will. I have written him from Canada. He is expecting us."

John adds, "We do know what we're doing. Thank you for everything. We'll be fine."

John has outfitted the car with a pillow and comforter for me. In the last couple of days, he has had to learn to drive on the left side of the road, with the steering wheel on the right side of the car. He heads north and I waft in and out of sleep, hearing his descriptions of the landscapes we're passing through. We spend the first night in a roadside motel in Pontefract. I have a moment of anxiety, my confidence falters and John calls the front desk. The manager is helpful and says if anything happens in the night, we are to call and he'll have a cab sent immediately to drive us to the hospital in Leeds.

~~~~

Night passes without event and morning brings the reassurance we'll soon be meeting Dr. Wheeler. Reaching the outskirts of Edinburgh, John pulls into a gas station. He pores over the city map, locates the hospital, drives through the city navigating each roundabout with steely determination, and finally, with a whoop as triumphant as an explorer discovering a new land, enters the hospital parking lot. The receptionist listens carefully to our request and says, "Dr. Wheeler is right here in the hospital. You go and have some tea in the room just over there and he'll be out in a minute to meet you."

Dr. Wheeler had been recommended to me by an acquaintance in the United States. A doctor I'd been in touch with in London had also recommended him, and while I was in Reading, the doctors had said I'd be in expert hands with him. "The 'General' is a teaching hospital and Dr. Wheeler heads a lupus clinic out of it."

He comes into the tea-room a few minutes later and looking expectantly around the room, smiles and inquires, "Ms. Clarke?" Identifying ourselves, we shake hands and I feel my whole body relax. *We'll be all right now.*

"I'm sorry, I'm just about to give a lecture. Would you mind my very capable partner taking over your care for today?"

Dr. Wheeler would only be working with someone as knowledgeable about lupus as himself.

"That'll be fine."

Later in the week, I return to the hospital for my second appointment. This time, Dr. Wheeler is out of town lecturing. The third time he's available, and I'm offered an appointment with him, but by now I'm comfortable with his associate, Dr. Armand, and decide to continue seeing him. He draws vials of my blood himself while I tell my tale of the manifestations and eventual diagnosis of lupus to three or four medical students who are my constant audience this year. One day, Dr. Armand says, "Systemic Lupus Erythematosus is the most elegant of all the autoimmune diseases." He proceeds to explain why. I don't register his intricate medical explanation. I just hear the words, "most elegant!" It sounds like a kind of honour. *No run of the mill disease for me. My disease is the most elegant of all the autoimmune diseases!*

We are aware that my serum creatinine level may have risen because the chicken pox virus has kicked my immune system into overdrive, resulting in a kidney flare. If so, we will surely reboard a plane and return home. Our first month in Scotland has an undercurrent of worry. This waiting game is familiar to all lupus patients with kidney disease. Three weeks later, my serum creatinine returns to its normal level — the anti-viral medications I'd been taking had been the cause of the elevated reading. I spend the rest of the year symptom free and healthy. *Wolf is an ocean away. Is the distance too daunting, even for him? Or is he just resting, worn out from his own vigilance.*

~~~~

This sabbatical, we find ourselves living in the lap of luxury. We've rented a condominium on the outskirts of Edinburgh, in a village called Colinton. It's furnished with antiques, a washer and dryer, a microwave and a gas fireplace. It has a shower *and* bathtub, a telephone, and every dish, utensil, pot and pan we could ever need. Things really are different from the France sabbatical; this year, John writes on a laptop computer he bought just before we left Canada.

I recover surprisingly quickly from the chicken pox, and once again, we establish a daily ritual in a new landscape. Rising early, we sit and chat over coffee before starting to work. John then settles in at his desk in the living room and I cover a large table in the same room with plastic. After each painting session, I clean up the paint and pastel dust and remove the plastic so we can eat our supper on the table at night. We usually work until noon, have lunch and then head up walking into the Pentlands, over Torduff Hill. Sometimes we pack a lunch and walk farther over the hills covered in fall-brown heather to a village named Currie.

I find a benevolent sun in Scotland, a sun often diffused by mist or cloud. I walk midday, protected still with sunscreen, but without anxiety. The land has a burnished, ancient feel to it. I sense the history of the place and its people each time I walk. It becomes a meditative experience for me, one that is punctuated with great gusts of gale-force winds that wake me up and get me moving. The whipping air tears everything up, dust flies and my eyes smart. When it dies down, there are the Pentlands, its grasses combed smooth and clean, and once again, that diffused, benevolent sun.

There is a spareness to the landscape. Few trees and a close, almost hard, textured surface of heather, bracken and gorse. Close up, the vegetation forms a weblike intricacy of colour and form that from a distance seems a smooth and burnished surface. I want to include all this in my paintings and catch the rhythm of the wind, to create a kind of visual music.

I want to burnish the watercolour paper, do to it what the sun, rain, and wind does naturally to the land over time. To get that feeling of age into the paper: a patina.

I begin applying paint with my usual technique — wet on wet — but now I allow the paint to dry and then apply another layer of paint on top of the last one. I don't want these paintings to float over the surface of the paper. I want them to have weight. This is a different landscape I'm painting. But it's all wrong. The paintings become overworked, opaque and flat-looking. Lifeless. The very antithesis of what I want.

~~~~

I'm lying in the bedroom after another unsuccessful morning painting. Trying to settle down and have a nap. But I can't sleep because I'm trying to figure out what to do. Plus I've propped the painting up so I can see it from where I'm lying which ensures that I'll never settle down. *I need a breakthrough.* I stare at it. *There's got to be something.* A thought occurs. I jump out of bed, carefully pick up the work and head for the bathroom. I scour the bathtub, then fill it with cool water. I lay the painting down, submerge it. Pick up a sponge, press the paper to the bottom of the tub and lightly stroke it. The water is soon murky brown. I lift the paper up and examine it. *Yes.* All the excess paint has washed off but the staining colours have remained fixed. The paint is transparent again. My heart quickens. I carry the painting, dripping, out of the bathroom and back into the living room. John looks up at me quizzically, then continues working. I lay the paper down on my painting table, pick up a black conte crayon and make a few sweeping lines. The conte glides smoothly and is very black on the wet paper. I pick up a white conte crayon, turn it on its side and make a few sweeps beside the black lines, over the paint. The look is dry and textured even though the paper is wet and the white conte makes the colours even brighter. I rummage around in my box and find what I'm looking for: a soft, wheat-coloured pastel. I lightly draw a few lines over the painting. *Yes.* The pastel glides easily, making a blurry line. I turn it on its side and gently swipe an area of the painting. The pastel catches on the raised nub of the textured paper. Dipping a brush in Lamp Black, I press my thumb and forefinger to the base of the brush, fanning the hairs out and separating them into clumps. When I brush a few experimental strokes over the pastel, the waterpaint mixes with the dry pigment and becomes smooth and opaque where the clumps make contact. I continue sponging small areas, reapplying pastel and paint until I'm satisfied with the feel of it. The painting is becoming more and more layered, opaque in some areas, still transparent in others. Finally, I stand up on a chair (it would drip if I propped it vertically) so I can view the finished work from a distance. *Yes.* A few days later, I title the painting *Into the Whitening Night.* It's my "breakthrough" painting.

~~~~

For the next five months I continue painting with this process of washing off, adding line with conte, adding pastel and more paint, rubbing and blending with brushes, sponges and fingers. If I go too far or work too long and the painting loses its life, I just take it into the

Figure 4
Into the Whitening Night, 1994/95

Figure 5
Windswept: Pentlands, 1994/95
Mixed media

Figure 6
Pentlands, Thickening, 1994/95
Mixed media

Figure 7
Meditation on a Gaelic Dream #1, 1994/95

Figure 8
Meditation on a Gaelic Dream #3, 1994/95
Mixed Media

Figure 9
Benevolent Sun
1994/95
Mixed Media

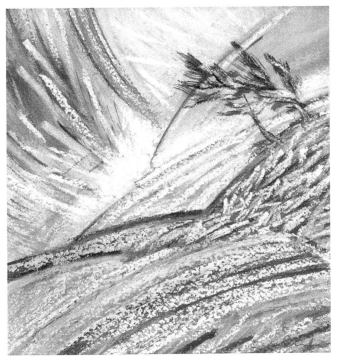

Figure 10
Two Trees Yielding
1994/95
Mixed Media

bathroom, scrub the whole thing down and start again. It's not an especially economical or even practical way to paint, but it gives me the finish I want: a layered and burnished ground.

~~~~

Some days we take the bus into town and explore Edinburgh. We walk up and down Princes Street with throngs of people, eventually leave this busyness for the next parallel street, Rose Street. It's closed to cars: narrow, cobbled, and dotted with pubs and unusual shops; one is a western shop and sells cowboy boots and big Texas-style hats. This seems particularly incongruous in a city that has a kilted Scot blowing a bagpipe on every major inter-section corner! Eventually, we cross another intersection to the third parallel street, George Street, and go into James Thin's Books to browse and have coffee: a tradition practised in Scottish books stores long before Chapters and Starbucks joined forces in Canada, offering patrons books and coffee. In Scotland, though, tea is the preferred beverage, and shortbread the staple accompa-niment.

Other days we walk from Colinton into the city, through the park known as The Meadows, until we reach the university, and while John uses the computers or library, I browse in my favourite art supply store. We go to an afternoon movie or end up at La Florentine for coffee and a croissant, or walk down the cobbled, winding road into Grass Market, the medieval district of town. This is the home of the Last Drop pub where, according to local lore, criminals were permitted a last drink before being led in shackles out to the "hanging square", to the crowds of cheering, jeering citizens waiting for the entertainment to begin.

We can smell the pungent aroma of cheese in the air and never fail to look in at the cheese shop, at the huge rounds of white, cream, orange, and even brown cheeses, piled high, filling the small shop to the brim. Sometimes we go in, taste the sample of the day and buy a wedge to take home.

I nap later than usual in the day because we only have about six hours of daylight and we want to make good use of the time. We eat supper late and listen to the radio, play cards, write letters, or read. We congratulate ourselves on our discipline and know this is no small thing, working this daily schedule. It takes stamina and focus. Especially when you don't know anyone but each other. Think about it. Twenty-four hours a day, seven days a week, for weeks on end with only your partner to do things with or talk to! How *did* we do it? John takes one last walk around the block at night to have a cigarette, and while he's gone I huddle into our electric blanket and listen to the winds, "the Westerlies", howling their power over the land.

It's really hard to meet people. We feel our neighbours regard our friendliness as slightly suspect. *Who are these two people who don't seem to know anyone, and are definitely not working at any job?* Our daily stop at the convenience store a block from our condo becomes a social event. We discuss the weather with the owner.

Craig, a friend of ours John teaches with in Vernon, is spending the year in Sterling working on his doctoral thesis. Occasionally he takes the bus and meets us at Bewley's for breakfast. John and he select "fried everything" from the buffet counter, heaping their plates with ham, bacon, potatoes, eggs and toast while I (sensible *moi*) choose fruit and yogurt, granola and toast. Craig tells us how work is going on his thesis and anything interesting that's going on in the communal grad students' house he lives in. We all "whinge" about how expensive everything is. Craig says, "I guess I won't be taking that holiday to Greece in February." Jeanne, his wife, comes to visit him in Sterling just before Christmas with their young son, Callum, and Craig takes us all to visit friends of his in St. Andrews. Jan and Jack welcome us into their home and feed us mounds of holiday goodies. We talk and laugh with their sons and are so happy to be included in this family gathering.

February, 1995

We drive the green Volvo south to Nine Mile Burn. We leave the car and walk past several sheep rooting around in a field of mud and turnips. The mud sucks at our hiking boots. We can see five black windblown trees far away in the distance. We walk the base of a hill, climbing gradually over a rolling, golden landscape. Its grasses are combed to a smooth burnished surface by the winds, again and again, here too. When we reach the trees, closeup they appear fossilized, permanently in motion and yet not a breath of air moving.

We curve around the base of the hill and see a stone farmhouse and green fields misted and pastoral-perfect in the valley below.

We're climbing higher now. A man and his young son pass us on the path. They're out for their Sunday "hill-walk" over the far range to the next village. His wife will be waiting there with the car and they're going for chips at the local pub. We can see bicyclists in green and pink fluorescent outfits peddling straight up the side of the highest mountain to the right of us. The man explains they are in training for a competition.

"Have a good day then!"

We climb up and up to an area that is coloured rust and dull purple with bracken and winter heather. A lean, fit and elderly woman jogs past us going the other direction.

We angle off and begin to walk back over the hill, still climbing, in the direction of our car. It feels like we are walking over the curve of the earth. The wind is blowing hard now, and the sun is bright, but I am perfectly protected with a hood and scarf covering all but my eyes, sunscreen and gloves. We reach the top of the hill and look down into the valley and see a panorama of golds and greens and brownish purples, and our car, a green speck in the distance.

John starts down the hill first, and in a minute I call to him. He turns slowly, bracing himself against the wind, and I click the camera. "Are you ready for some chips now?"

"You bet!"

~~~~

I feel as strong as I felt years ago, tree planting, before the symptoms of lupus started to occur. These daily hikes up, over, and down hills have made my leg muscles and lungs strong. I am thirty-nine years old. Standing in the snow in my hiking boots on the top of the Knock of Crieth one day, I feel invincible, every cell in my body alive and well: blood rich, bones dense, nerves steady. I take deep breaths and slowly turn round, looking over miles and miles of misted Scottish farmland. Hundreds of sheep dot the fields; the ones closest to me are munching grass, or curled up on the ground, sleeping. No one, beast or human, is concerned here.

There is no Wolf here.

~~~~

We cross the wide expanse of lawn, pass the familiar metal sculptures and walk up the wide steps into the Modern Art Gallery. An attendant welcomes us to the exhibition and hands us a brochure. We turn, walk the few steps to the main exhibition room and are brought up short. I gasp. We can't, literally, go any farther than the edge of the entranceway to the room.

I am looking at approximately 40,000 six to eight inch, bisque-fired, primitively formed clay figures. They fill the gallery wall to wall and all face me; the closest is three or four inches from the toe of my hiking boots. 40,000 sets of eyes, small holes poked in clay, are looking at me. John and I don't say a word. I feel something human, alive here. I think I can hear or feel the sound of thousands of hearts beating. *What is it? Is it hope? Hope that as human beings on this earth, we'll make the right decisions for ourselves and for the world? Or am I seeing my own soul mirrored back at me?*

These simple figures hold my gaze and thoughts until I become aware of a slight noise behind me. I turn and see four or five people shifting on their shoes, waiting patiently for me to move away from the entranceway so they can view the exhibition.

John and I move away, go and stand near the door to the outside grounds and watch as several couples, a small cluster of students, an elderly gentleman on his own take their turn, step up to the entranceway and see "Field For The British Isles" by Anthony Gormley for the first time.

Later at home, I reread the brochure that tells me the figures for "Field" were made by about a hundred people living in St. Helens. Gormley stressed from the beginning an important dimension of his work was that families — children, parents and grandparents — work together, side by side, while they formed these 40,000 figures. *Was it the beating of their hearts I heard and felt, their connections to one another, their hopes reaching out to me through these simple shapes they had fashioned from clay? Tomorrow, Anthony Gormley's speaking at the gallery. I'll take the bus back to the gallery and hear him.*

~~~~

This year in Edinburgh I view exhibition after exhibition: all kinds of work by all kinds of artists in all manner of galleries: huge, gilt-framed 18th-century portraits in the "red room" of The Mound gallery, drawings by Michaelangelo and light-filled paintings by the French Impressionists at the City Art Gallery. I view contemporary work by Scottish, English, Aboriginal Australian, European artists, installations by art students, an exhibition of hundreds of tiny collages built under plastic CD cases in another, small, artist-run gallery.

I look at art portraying the underbelly of Edinburgh, the side portrayed in the movie *Trainspotting*. John and I get glimpses of the real thing in the evidence of drug addiction left in public washrooms and parks, as we walk by the lone person chattering with craziness and cold, huddled in a dark corner of a crooked passageway to High Street. We see it in and around the train station, young people looking at us vacantly or with contempt, like we're from another world, which we are: the world of privilege. We're aware of a thick skin of wealth and conventionality in Edinburgh that covers a raw nerve of poverty and everything that comes with that. I doubt if we flew into Edinburgh for a few days, we would see or notice any of this. We see it because we walk every nook and cranny, every street of this city, day after day, for months. We see it because we walk with our eyes lifted from the pavement and have the time to see it.

~~~~

In March, when naturalized crocuses bloom orange and purple throughout city parks, we pack up the Volvo and leave Edinburgh for our much-anticipated return to Strasbourg. This return is full of the confidence of familiarity; our friends are all we remember them to be and Strasbourg just as exciting. John goes into the little *tabac* shop where he'd bought his cigarettes seven years ago and is greeted with, *"Ah, le Canadienne! Bonjour, Monsieur, Comment allez-vous?"* from the same smiling face of the same woman who'd sold him his cigarettes in 1988.

"Tres bien, merci, Madame. Et vous?"

Continuing our stroll through Petite France, we finally see our old apartment. "John, look! There she is. She still lives there. Quick! Walk up ahead of me, turn around, I'll take a picture of you and get her in the background."

Yes, it's our lady of the night, and she's leaning out her window chatting to people passing by. *I wonder if our furniture's still up there in her flat.*

Near the end of our stay, at a dinner party hosted by Christiane's sister, a newly-met couple offer us the use of their summer place in Rustrel, a tiny village in Provence, for as long as we want. We are going to Arles, to see where Vincent Van Gogh lived and painted the last two years of his life.

March, 1995

We drive south through the French Alps and cross over to
Berne, Switzerland, to see Paul Klee's work. John and I
find the gallery easily and walk separately through
different rooms. I stop at a painting that has orange and
yellow oval-shaped clouds floating in a grey-blue sky.
There's a mountain and a lake with chunky orange and
gold boats. *It's whimsical. Child-like.*

Close by is a long, horizontal painting. In this work,
Klee has drawn purposeful-looking black lines over a
mostly pink background. Some of the lines look like
music symbols. *There's a face and a flute. They look like
hierogyphics. Hmmm.* I look more closely at the canvas. *He's
painted the whole thing on burlap. That's how he gets that rough,
textured finish.*

I move on to another painting. This one is painted on
burlap, too, but . . . *look at that. He's glued pieces of newspaper
onto the burlap and washed a thinner paint over them so you can
still see the printed words. I could try this out with the kids back
at the gallery, in Vernon.*

After an hour or so, John and I leave the gallery, find
a café where we eat two of the worst hamburgers we've
ever tasted and for which we pay seventeen dollars each.
We have to go to the bank twice during our three-hour
sojourn in Switzerland. Needless to say, we are relieved
to drive back into France.

Still heading south, we reach the lowlands and follow
a winding road through acres and acres of lavender fields.
The plants are small and green. Just getting started. As we

get closer to our village, the earth changes to a reddish-brown and keeps getting lighter and lighter in colour. We come around a bend and see a postcard-perfect farm-house set in a field of lavender shoots. The farmhouse seems lit from within, not by electricity but naturally, by the golden-red glow of the earth it's made of, reaching out to touch the last rays of the day's sun.

A few more twists and turns in the road later, we reach the peach-toned village of Rustral and easily locate the summer house. We spend the week exploring the towns around us. The texture of the buildings is dry, chalky, worn by time and weather, softened to mellow hues of pink, orange, wheat and creamy beige. In Avignon, we walk around the huge papal monastery, and hear a voice singing, *"Sur le pont d'Avignon"*. Looking up, we see a small boy on a balcony. He's marching back and forth and looking our way, singing as loudly as he can, so that we'll be sure to see him. We wave and clap our hands. Bravo! A command performance!

Another day we drive to Gordes. I've seen this land-scape before — in Cezanne's paintings. The road to the village winds up a hill. Gordes is perched on top, all angles and soft-edged geometric shapes. The buildings are made of creamy-grey earth and stone. The restaurants aren't open yet, so we enter a little bar which surprisingly is, and have coffee and a croissant. There are three or four locals there, too, who ignore us. They're used to thousands of strangers visiting their village and couldn't care less about us. We find the gallery that holds Vasarely's paintings but don't go in because neither of us is much interested in his work. All that formality of hard line and repetitious geometric shape.

We save Arles until mid-week. We park the car outside the city, walk into the town, round the coliseum, and continue our way along winding, narrow streets. Much to our disappointment, we discover the museum for Van Gogh's work closed for renovations. Coming across a small restaurant, we enter and order pizza and an unfortunate liver salad. (I had mistranslated the menu.) When the owner finds out we're Canadians, he jokes about the runner, Ben Johnson, and mimes sticking a needle into his arm. The locals around us laugh at his antics. We join in half-heartedly and are glad to leave. *These people would have laughed at Vincent, too.* According to a book I had read a long time ago — in high school, I think — Vincent was actually stoned by the locals, jeered at as he returned home from a day of painting his soul out under the hot Provence sun.

I stand across the street, survey the entire square and turning back to look at the restaurant once again, think, *Café at Night* by Vincent van Gogh. *This could be it.* I store up the image, note the physical details of the square in my head. The teacher in me is taking notes, too. I now have a first-hand description of Arles to give the students back at home.

~~~~

The locals are treating us with disdain, like "ugly tourists", and John and I are both in "high dudgeon" about that. A waiter in Avignon had charged us double for coffee, and when John challenged him on it we got that blank, closed-off stare we'd seen other travellers receive but whose rude behaviour we thought had warranted it. Surely, *we* don't fall into that category. The waiter had looked at us like he hadn't understood a word John said — the final insult being that John had spoken to him in French!

Even in our beloved Strasbourg, in our favourite *chocolatiere* by the Cathedral, I'd been charged triple for our purchase and only had the money returned, jammed hard into my hand with a sneer, after I'd asked to speak to the manager. We'd never had one instance like this the entire year we'd lived in Strasbourg on John's first sabbatical and not one this past year in Edinburgh. But we hadn't been tourists in either place, then. We'd been living there and the locals can just smell the difference. I know I can, back home in the Okanagan.

~~~~

There are other things getting to us, too.

"Man, listen to that wind!"

"The mistral."

"Yeah. Here, I'll tie the shutter with this old rope."

Back in bed, John says, "It just broke the rope." He gets up again, reties it, and finds another piece of rope to double secure the first piece. Then he's back in bed. "Shit, there it goes again." He drags every chair in the room to the window and lines them up against the shutters. Finally, the shutters stop banging and everything is secure. We can still hear the wind howling outside, but eventually we go to sleep.

Next morning, John says, "We've gotta get out of here. We're broke, living on credit cards. We don't speak French and the French obviously don't want us here. What if the car breaks down? How am I going to figure out how to get it fixed? 'Cause you know it'll be me that'll have to figure it out. What about the lupus? Every time we go to a new town, the first thing we do is locate the hospital. I don't think one person speaks English here and we don't really speak their language. How would we be able to explain anything? I just want to get out of here. Today. Let's just pack up and head over to Aix-en-Provence. We can stay there a couple of days and then drive up through Burgundy. We'll stay in a new town each night and just take our chances with the ferry. We can be in London in a few days."

Damn it. You actually thought you could just get in a car with John and take off to the south of France without a care in the world. Wolf doesn't need to be here in person to mess with our ability to enjoy this trip. He just has to plant the idea of his presence in our heads. He's been worrying our minds, and now, I can hear him laughing. Mocking us.

The bottom line is that we haven't been able to shake a lingering vulnerability caused by the trauma of the chicken pox. Things could happen. Things that could be very serious, involving the lupus. And we really are "strangers in a strange land". We feel nervous, unprotected. Neither of us has admitted to the other our anxieties about that, but it's been undermining most of our stay in Provence.

Within an hour we've packed and cleaned the house. We lock the door, drop the key into an envelope which we'll mail to our generous hosts later today in Aix-en-Provence, and drive off down the road.

April, 1995

John and I return from Europe two months before we'd planned. It's good to be home, safe and sound. The summer is busy, full of visiting friends and relatives and making small improvements to the house and garden. Five years ago, we'd bought another old house with a bigger garden. We have endless projects we'd been putting off so we could afford the sabbatical in Edinburgh and now begin working on these.

Georgia had died the summer before we went away and we decide, now, to get another dog. We go see a litter of ten female Lhasa Apsos and come home with a black-eyed ball of toffee-coloured fur that fits easily into the palm of John's hand. She is the exact opposite of Georgia in size and temperament. She thinks she's the Supreme Ruler of our family, whereas Georgia loved to please and was happiest with her head pressed against one of our legs. We now have a walking, yipping, Gund-toy puppy and we name her Finnegan.

John and I return to work in the fall and I finish up and frame the twenty-five paintings I'd done in Edinburgh for my exhibition in February. The fall is full and balanced. I feel healthy and fit. We had hill-walked almost every day in Scotland and now, back in Vernon, my friend Linda and I are swimming lengths regularly in the community pool. I'm glad to be back with the kids in the Education Program. I have an all-round sense of well-being.

February, 1996

The title of my exhibition is *A Burnished Land — paintings of Scotland*. Because part of my job at the public art gallery is to tour elementary school-age classes through each exhibition, I am in the unique position of having a captive audience for my own work. For four weeks I get to blab on about my paintings and our year away. The students are full of questions and ideas, curious about all kinds of things. I get them talking about specific works and thoroughly enjoy every minute of our discussions. Shamelessly!

I can't resist including my favourite critique of my work by a student in Grade three:

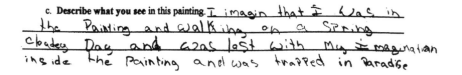

c. Describe what you see in this painting. I imagin that I was in the Painting and walking on a Spring clodey Day and was lost with my imaginatian inside the Painting and was trapped in Paradise

If you were going to be "trapped" anywhere, Paradise would be the place to be.

July, 1996, Vernon

The phone rings and John picks it up. He murmurs a few words, places the receiver down, and looks up at me, stricken.

"David McAvoy died last night. Your mom just heard. It was his heart."

"Oh no. No. No. Not David."

Dr. McAvoy had cared for me for the last sixteen years. He was in his early fifties when he died. Aside from the constancy of his expert professional care, I miss the assurance and just the sound of his big booming voice and the kindness in those brown eyes. Whenever I was flaring, it seemed to take forever and many different drugs to get my blood pressure down to an acceptable reading. Dr. McAvoy's own frustration was palpable; I remember one such incident during a flare:

I'm sitting in Dr. McAvoy's office and looking at his landscape photographs on the wall while he takes my blood pressure. I glance back at him as he releases the air pump and we both watch the monitor.

He says, "Come on. Come on. Damn it."

I'm in the middle of a kidney flare. I'm on three different kinds of medication for high blood pressure and they're not working. My blood pressure is still too high. Dr. McAvoy is willing it to drop. His concentration is total. He tries it again. No luck.

"Jude, I'm going to double the accupril. We've got to get your blood pressure down."

"Is it caused by the kidney disease or the prednisone?"

"Probably both."

I sit at the corner of his desk as he scribbles out the new prescription. He looks up at me with such kindness and sympathy, I burst into tears. He says, "Are you doing all right, Jude?"

"Yes, I'm OK. It's just so hard sometimes, all of this. It's mostly the drugs, you know. I have such a hard time on the prednisone."

"I know. I'm so sorry you're going through all of this."

"Thanks, David. I'll see you next week."

He is scribbling down notes in my file as I leave his office.

~~~~

I make an appointment for John and I to see my GP, Dr. McAvoy's wife, Dr. Lindsay. We want to express our sympathy and tell her how much David has meant to us over the years.

Eventually, we discuss other internists in town. She sets up an appointment for me with a Dr. Bouma. I then make a call to Vancouver to set up an appointment with Dr. Ballard, my nephrologist. I haven't actually seen him since just before we went to Edinburgh. I'm told he has retired. Suddenly, I feel really at sea. I'm going to have to establish a relationship with two new doctors. I had formed trusting, personable relationships with Dr. McAvoy and Dr. Ballard over the years. They knew my medical history. I didn't want to have to start over, be defined by a file containing twenty years of lab results — hundreds of numbers charting the clinical path of the disease. That the doctor knows and cares about the human being he or she is treating is synonymous in my mind with the best medical care. I think it's especially important to a person living with a chronic disease.

~~~~

Dr. Ballard had always first asked about my life when I saw him. I sent him a note, once, written on one of my water-colour cards. The next time I was in his office I saw that he had tacked the card to his bulletin board. When he learned that John is a writer, he asked if he might read some of his work.

I always felt like a person rather than a disease sitting in his office. Even though he was a kidney specialist, he approached my kidney involvement as just one part of a larger problem. He addressed lupus as the *systemic* disorder that it is. He was as concerned about the pinpoint cataracts in my eyes, the butterfly rash across my nose and cheeks and my periodic chest pain as he was about the condition of my kidneys. He was the one who asked if I thought the shock of my father's death had affected the lupus in any way.

Because of all this, I could forgive him the time he wagged his finger at me after I'd asked a question and said, "Now, I have to keep some things to myself, you know."

No, I don't know, and I want the answer to my question right now.

I was too intimidated to say this out loud at that point, but I'd have no problem saying it now. Otherwise, Dr. Ballard was forthright and compassionate, an exemplary doctor in his thoroughness. In retrospect, I realize that in the process of examining and questioning me, he was also educating me about lupus. Each time I'd see him, he would ask me many questions, always the same ones over the years. In time, I began to see that the answers I gave to these questions were not only giving me a detailed picture of the clinical effect lupus was having on me — they were also revealing the manifestations of lupus I wasn't experiencing. That, in itself, was a positive lift.

~~~~

My first appointment with Dr. Bouma is a success. He has a quiet, relaxed air about him. He speaks thoughtfully, in a way I find calming, and he admits he's not an expert on lupus, so he'll be in close contact with my nephrologist in Vancouver. It is everything I want to hear. I do a little research on my own and find out he's here with his young family, which means I can be reasonably sure Vernon isn't just a temporary work location. People with chronic illness don't want their doctors to leave town. Also, I'm pretty sure he's younger than me, which means I can probably count on him not retiring before *I* do.

~~~~

I call a friend who had recently been head nurse of the children's kidney unit in a hospital in Vancouver. "I need a nephrologist who is very good professionally, but I also want one who will answer my questions. In detail. Someone who is easy to talk to, who will recognize that I want to be involved in and informed about all aspects of my treatment." I laugh and add, "You know, I want *everything!*" My friend replies, "Well, that would be Dr. Penn, then." So Dr. Penn it becomes.

I find the opening minutes of my first meeting with him disconcerting. We enter his office. There on his desk is my thick file, which I've had sent over from Dr. Ballard's office. The file is unopened. He asks, "Now what is it that has brought you here?"

He doesn't even know I have lupus. We're going to have to start from scratch.

I'm anxious but soon begin to relax. *He's asking the questions. He's starting a new file with his own notes.* I throw in personal information about my life. I establish the fact I'm an artist. I have the strangest feeling. The whole time he's asking the questions, I'm observing what he says and how he says it. I feel like *I'm* interviewing *him*, to see if I think he can do the job. I feel confident. This is a sure sign I've changed. I'm not going to be a passive participant in this relationship. I now want a doctor/patient relationship where the two of us will work together.

I know he's the doctor for me when in the middle of a serious talk about kidney disease, he blurts out, "Excuse me, but I just have to show you this." He jumps up, takes something that looks like a small human head made out of clay from his bookshelf, hands it to me, and asks, "What do you think this is?" The following discussion about art confirms that this doctor is personable as well as highly qualified.

I ask him, too, "Dr. Penn, have any of your patients ever told you they feel smarter when they're on prednisone?"

"No," he says, "But I did hear about a patient, once, who said he'd found Jesus while he was taking the drug!"

"Really! Did he keep Jesus after the prednisone was reduced?"

"I have no idea."

~~~~

Dr. McAvoy had managed all of my lupus-related and non-related medical problems. I had only seen my GP, Dr. Lindsay, once a year for my annual physical. She knew I had lupus, of course, but we rarely discussed it in any depth during our appointments. Now she becomes more involved.

One day, I tell her I want to visualize my kidneys working properly. So I need to know what a healthy kidney looks like and how it functions. She responds by drawing a quick sketch and gives me a verbal explanation. She then draws and describes what happens when my body turns on itself, causing inflammation, and then protein to "spill" from my kidneys. I catch phrases like "nest of blood vessels", "cross-referencing", "plugging and leaking". It's all very technical so I simply imagine my kidneys as two leaky bird's nests.

I'll help the medications fix the problem by mentally weaving twigs and grasses into the nests until they're sealed properly. Then I'll have "safe nests", or rather, kidneys that won't leak protein.

March 1996

I've been back working for six months at the gallery after returning from Edinburgh, when a friend of mine pops in one day. She has chronic fatigue and fibromyalgia and we're talking about work and self-definition. I hear myself saying, "I feel like I don't have anything to prove anymore." Just like that. It's sneaked up on me and I hadn't realized it until now. Now I'm working simply because I love the job. I realize I'm healthy, fulfilled, at ease. I'd had an exhibition of my Scotland paintings just the month before. I'm feeling slim and fit. I've put henna in my hair!

Things seem fine.

I finish work in June, at the same time the schools have their summer break. I then have the time and energy to paint, and this summer I'm especially inspired, looking forward to it. I've set up an exhibition date for new work for the following November. I get into a daily routine fairly quickly: early morning walk, paint for three or four hours, lunch, snooze, garden, visit friends or swim in the lake.

The paintings come along well, and by the end of the summer I'm ready for my exhibition. Just a few more small ones to do in the fall and then the framing. Throughout the summer, we keep an eye on my lab-test results. I do them every month instead of every three months because there are a few indications that things might be percolating. I'm not unduly concerned, though. I feel good and have been accomplishing a lot.

That's the problem. I'm now functioning as well and as productively as a person without a chronic disease. I'm managing it all. I don't see the absolute rigidity of my life. In order to accomplish these things, I have to be on top of everything, all the time. Even my afternoon naps aren't relaxing. They're more like a quick fix, something to assuage the surface fatigue but nothing that can reach the deeper exhaustion building underneath.

At night I drop into bed, spent. This exhaustion doesn't warn me or point out the obvious; I'm doing too much. It seems I have to relearn my limits, time and time again. I mistake all this productivity for health. I have a sense of exhilaration. I've reached a point where I feel a great deal of satisfaction in what I'm accomplishing; I feel I'm fulfilling the goals I've set for myself. I don't see how drained I am. I don't see that what I think is just me living a normal life is me pushing myself every hour of the day to have a life that isn't realistic for me. I've been pushing myself for so long, have become so used to testing myself since the day I was first diagnosed with lupus, that I can't let up. It's like my mind and body are set on remote, programmed by me, to fulfill all the expectations that I, in my youth and terrible fear, had set for myself.

I was *ashamed* to be ill. I have an immune system that turns on itself, attacks its own healthy tissues and organs randomly. Instead of giving myself compassion, I chose to not only turn my back but also to actively punish myself for what I saw as a great weakness of character. Double whammy. It wasn't that I thought I had done some terrible thing to deserve this disease. No. The shame was that I thought I had somehow *allowed* myself to get sick. That I could have prevented it and didn't.

This was my starting point. From here, I measured everything I did and didn't do, judged it all harshly. I didn't stand a chance. Every way I turned, I became more and more entangled in self-judgement, in what I saw as my failure to cope well with this disease. I couldn't find or even see my way out of this intricate web for such a long time.

While this makes me sad in retrospect, I know too that, in part, this is what kept me going. I was determined to do things in spite of this disease. I did things *because* I had lupus. This is the redeeming aspect of illness: you go along, you live your life as best you can. You find ways to cope. And one day you realize that the disease isn't just the all-consuming, fearsome Wolf you thought it was. It's also a gift; one that has allowed you to see other bigger and brighter truths in life, and to find truths in yourself and others that wouldn't have been found without it.

It took a long time for this to become clear to me. It took another kidney flare, five years after the last one.

July, 1997

My friend Ronee and I are sitting in the living room of her house which is perched high on a hill overlooking Okanagan Lake. The living room also serves as her studio, and we're looking at three large paintings resting on easels, that are in-progress. These paintings form a triptych and are of an apple orchard. They're representational with a definite foreground, middle ground and background. Ronee has painted the scene from a perspective that makes you feel, looking at the painting, that you're lying in the grass looking up the slope of a hill. The foreground of grass, earth and fallen apples is immediate to the viewer's eye. You have a feeling of great intimacy with the land.

My friend isn't afraid of red. She uses it as an underbase and continues using it as she builds her compositions, interspersing chunky, expressive brushstrokes of red with green and orange with blue — natural complements. These paintings jump with life, draw you in, make you want to pick up that fallen apple on the ground and crunch your teeth into its crisp, juicy flesh. Ronee paints slowly with great attention to detail. Much of her work is symbolic and personal. These orchard paintings are symbolic, too, but less overtly so. The oldest orchards in the Okanagan are slowly disappearing and she wants to "catch" this one — not far from her house — before it's gone. These paintings are recording history, and more subtly, loss. I can feel it when I look at them.

~~~~

There is a painting in my studio, zipped up in my black portfolio. I painted it after I had recovered from a kidney flare. The painting is all red with black lines drawn into it. The lines, drawn with conte, are hard-edged and end sharply. They strike and cross over one another, break and tangle amidst a flaming red background. I remember that when I drew these lines, I gripped the conte so tightly it broke. I don't like to look at that painting. Every once in a while I unzip the portfolio and take a peek but I never bring it out to look at it full-on. I don't think about it very often, but when I do, I'm glad that I can't see it, that it is safely hidden, out of sight. But, of course, it's still there and I know that.

Red is the most psychologically potent of colours for me. I've come to associate it with lupus. It stands for the lethal, burning rays of the sun and the indelible marks Wolf leaves on my body: small, scaly lesions on my arms, tiny, inflamed capillaries on my face, or a broken blood vessel staining one eye red. It is the "butterfly rash" or in my case, the "butterfly flush" on my face which appears when I'm hot or very tired. It is the inflammation within my body. It is the remembrance of pain — the deep burn of arthritis, the searing breath of pericarditis.

I remember one occasion when I delighted in using the colour red.

September, 1960 (age 5)

I skip down the alley that leads to my friend Patty's house. She answers the knock on her door, and we set out, bubbling with excitement. Walking several blocks west towards town, we reach Pleasant Valley Road and turn onto it, walk a bit more until we reach "Lovers Lane", our favourite part of the journey. 'Lover's Lane,' is a dirt pathway covered with soft needles that have dropped from the ponderosa pines towering above us. The path is dark and mysterious. We always hope that we'll see some lovers strolling but we never do. (My sister, who is ten years old and knows about these things, tells me they're only seen at night.)

Finally reaching the church, Patty and I climb up the back stairs and enter the kindergarten room. My first memory of making art takes place here. It's very clear in my head. I am sitting at a big wooden table with the other kids. The teacher has set out several large boxes full of crayons. I pick up a black crayon and draw an image on the paper (I don't remember what it was). Then I pick up a red crayon and colour in a bit of the background. I can still see the white paper showing through so I press harder and now the red is dense, opaque and shiny. I keep filling in more and more of the background until it's completely covered. Then, I fill the space inside the black lines with red too. Now there's a fuzzy white space where I haven't coloured right up to the lines. I don't like it. So I scribble red right over the black lines, not caring if I lose the shape of whatever it is I've drawn. This feels really good. My heart does a little leap when the lines still show through. I didn't know you could do this. It was the first time I had coloured a drawing entirely with one colour and I felt brave and excited doing it. I loved looking at all that red.

August, 1997

Ronee and I spend the morning in Kelowna, buy art materials and wander through galleries. We have lunch with the education coordinator from the public art gallery, and driving home along the edges of first Wood and then Kalamalka Lake, we yack about everything under the sun. But there is something I'm not talking about.

When she drops me off, John is there, waiting in the kitchen.

"Dr. Bouma called. He said to come right up, as soon as you get home."

John and I are looking at each other. We both know what it is. My lab results have been warning us for the last two months. We hold each other for a moment. I fill Finnegan's water dish, John turns off the coffee, and we leave the house.

September, 1997

I've known for a week or so that the lupus is flaring and, as usual, my kidneys are involved. I've begun high-dose steroid treatment and am trying to get in a few more social events before the dreaded side effects begin. When they do, I will disappear into the sanctity of my home and the company of family and a few close friends.

The Wolf is resigned. She has known for a long time now that she will never — not in a million years — be able to outrun this fire.

~~~~

I'm at an art opening. There are hordes of people milling around because someone local is showing. Every time I turn, I bump into someone I know: an artist I haven't seen for a long time, a mother of a friend, a schoolteacher I've worked with, sometimes the teen-age daughter or son of a friend.

I'm animated talking to each one and soon begin to tire. The noise level and the heat in the crowded room combine to make me feel hot, flushed and hemmed in. I just want to get out. But I continue talking to each one and soon I find myself in a group of women I know casually. They're talking about the "run" they do every morning before getting the kids off to school or themselves off to work. One says, "Yeah, if I miss that morning run I've just got to go to the gym at noon because otherwise I feel crummy all day."

Another is talking about the family dinner party for fourteen she gave the night before. Her own family is going on a trip tomorrow so there'll be packing to be done and food to be organized later tonight. She wants to get an early start so she'll be up half the night getting ready.

I can feel my nemesis, Ms. Begrudge, taking over. At times like this, I divide the world in half. There is The Land of the Healthy on one side and The Land of the Sick on the other. I sure know which one I belong in. These are not my people. They're spontaneous, confident, and as blissfully unfettered as anyone can be who is physically healthy. I am sure they never think about parcelling out their energy, saving or using it all up.

At first, I begrudge not the women themselves, but the ease with which they nonchalantly make plans, change plans, the way they've been able to decide when to have children or for that matter not to have children. I am filled with dismay and anger. Then I begin to judge the women. They have no idea how privileged they are. They seem arrogant and unaware of life outside their own circle. Their club is exclusive. My judgement of them makes me smaller and smaller and more and more miserable. Soon, I am as small as I can be. I carry on listening for a few more minutes and then anxiously look around the room for my friend, Carole.

Carole is an artist with a health concern of her own right now. We meet a couple of times a week for tea and talk about our health briefly. That out of the way, we move on to art, to the home-schooling feat she has accomplished with all four of her daughters, and our plans for the future when we're both well again.

She walks by at this point and I grab her arm. I whisper, "Carole, are you ready to get out of here?"

Her nod lets me know we're both in the same land right now and we slip through the crowd and out the door.

September, 1997

I wish I could say this flare is different in every way from the last "nightmare flare" in 1992, but the truth is, my heart always sinks when I get the dreaded news that I'm flaring and the prednisone always does what it's going to do. I know now, from beginning to end, a flare means a year of my life. Complete havoc. But there *is* something different about this flare. After the initial disappointment, John and I begin to plan how to get through it in the most positive way. It becomes what we now call the "gift flare".

First, my sister and mom and I go on a shopping trip to Vancouver. We eat out every night at different restaurants — Greek, Thai, Indian — and have one of those rare shopping experiences only a woman can fully appreciate. We keep finding everything we want. We hit all the right stores. Everything fits. Everything looks great. The prices are all "right", and by the last day, we don't even care; we just bring out our credit cards and abandon all sense and practicality. We are on a spree.

At dinner one night, I remind Mom of one of our funniest clashes when I was a teenager.

She responds, shaking her head, "I thought you were the most spoiled child on the face of this earth!"

"But you had to admire my ingenuity and resourcefulness."

"I did," she allows, lifting a forkful of curry to her mouth, "I also couldn't believe your good luck. How it dropped right into your *lap!*"

September, 1969 (age 14)

"Well, I guess I'll just babysit when I have to, then, won't I?"

Mom replies, "Well, guess what? That's going to be right now because I'm cutting you off your clothing allowance as of this minute."

This allowance is twenty dollars a month. I can buy a new pair of GWG jeans or a couple of T-shirts and have enough money left over to keep me in pop, French fries and movies for the month.

"What do you mean?"

"Exactly what it sounds like it means."

"Well, fine then!"

Stomping down the hallway I hear, "And don't you dare slam that bedroom door one more time!" I slam the door as hard as I can. The plaster around the doorframe crackles, falls to the floor. I look in my bedroom mirror at my scowling face and dramatically mouth, "What a bitch!" realizing with a sinking feeling that the door slamming was a big mistake. I'm gonna be grounded Friday night, or have to get up really early Saturday morning to do extra yardwork.

Mom and I both like clothes. A lot. She knows this about me and I know it about her. Mom thinks she's got my "number" and I think I've got to figure out a way to outfit myself that doesn't cost anything. It's 1969. Things have been changing around the world and our small town is finally catching up. My friends and I start combing the thrift stores for anything natural, "far out", and old looking. I embroider flowers on my jeans and T shirts. I make a long jean skirt out of two pairs of old jeans I've cut and joined together with strips of burgundy velvet. Franny sews, with laces of leather she's cut by hand, a hipster suede miniskirt for me and I wear it with moccasins, tights, and a turtleneck. I throw my bra into the back of my closet and emerge a "liberated woman".

Not that I'd needed a bra in the first place.

One night there's a knock on our door and it's our next-door neighbour asking if I could take on a small job while he and his wife are away for six months. All I have to do is walk over and open his front door once a day. If I feel a blast of heat on my face, I'll know the furnace is working, but if I don't — if the air is cold — then I should phone his caretaker and let him know.

Our neighbour asks, "Would twenty dollars a month be all right?"
I grin at my mother. "It would be perfect," I say.

October, 1997

Back in Vernon, John and I drive a couple of times a week to a bakery/cafe in the country and have coffee and bring home scones and cinnamon buns and soup. *If I'm going to go on my usual food binge, I might as well do it with the good stuff, homemade food made by someone else.*

The second time I have my lab work done, the protein is almost completely gone from my urine and my serum creatinine has come down a little. It looks as if I'm not going to lose any more kidney function this time because the flare has been caught early.

Every morning I go on a walk. I'm determined to keep my weight down this flare. John gives me Dylan Thomas's "Fern Hill" to read and I see the neighbourhood through Thomas's eyes, try to imagine the words and rhythm he would have used to describe what is around me.

Dylan Thomas drank himself to death. I wonder what manner of Wolf was tracking him.

High-dose steroids heighten all my senses. Eating dinner with my sister one night, I look down at the steaming baked potato on my plate. Specks of pepper dot the buttered, glistening flesh like black stars against a creamy sky. *A constellation-in-reverse!* Taking a forkful and drawing it to my mouth, I catch the fragrance of rich

215

earth. I close my eyes and taste a piece of heaven sliding warm and silky down my throat.

When I describe this to my sister, Franny looks down at her plate and says sardonically, "Wow, Jude. I want my potato to taste like that. It doesn't, you know."

~~~~

Out walking one morning, I notice a cat steal out from behind a parked car just in front of me. I marvel at the beauty of the cat's sleek black shape moving against the red gleam of the car's bumper, as if I'm seeing something I've never — no, no one has ever — before seen. As the cat glides past me, I'm mesmerized by the slow switch of its tail until I blink and my hazel eyes shift to make contact with the cat's green ones. The feeling that some kind of shared "knowingness" has just passed between us startles me. I hear birds singing — not in their usual group twitter — but as if each is chirping its own song, a solo performance. I lean over and pluck a dewy shoot of clover from the edge of someone's lawn. I count only three leaves but it doesn't matter — its very *being* seems lucky to me this morning.

~~~~

I *am* conscious of the physical world in the way I've just described, normally. But, for a time when I'm taking high-dose steroids, I become even more acutely aware of physical detail. I feel more cognizant. I think I understand why I'm here on this earth. I get why we're all here. I couldn't articulate these revelations, even at the time I'm experiencing them, but neither do I feel the need to. It's a higher consciousness, for sure. (Or, some might say, something like an acid trip.)

I'm prepared for my early morning walks. I wear hiking boots with lots of support and tie them loosely so they won't bruise my feet. My route is level except for one small incline at the end. There will be no walking disaster this time. Wrong! After two and a half months, out walking one morning I feel a slight, spasm-like tug on my right Achilles' tendon and then a similar one on the other foot. Stepping out of bed the next day, I wince with pain when my foot hits the floor, wince again when the other foot bears weight. The prednisone has broken down the tissue in my tendons and I spend the next eight months hobbling from room to room, from the car to wherever I'm headed. I go for twice-weekly physiotherapy treatments. Taping my ankles offers some relief.

~~~~

I get up from my afternoon nap and hobble into the bathroom. I behold an apparition in the mirror. My hair is thick and wiry, and if I turn to each side and then onto my back while I'm sleeping my hair presses into a perfect rectangle which rises at least eight inches above my forehead. *I'm Don King. The boxing promoter. All I need is the black shades and the shiny jacket. This is too good to keep to myself.*

Without brushing my hair I leave the bathroom and meet John coming down the hall. I bow, extend my arm and say, "Hi, I'm Don King."

Immediately getting it, he roars with laughter, shakes my hand and says, "Nice ta meetcha, Don. Nice hairdo."

~~~~

John carries on fulfilling his obligations to his students and the college. He commutes an hour to and from work every day. Aside from marking and taking care of other paperwork, he attends meetings and sees students. His week includes three marathon days, each ending with a three-hour night class. He makes the necessary arrangements to bring in other writers for the college's reading series, picks them up at the airport and squires them around the valley. He does all of these things, but still feels like he's letting people down. He doesn't stay long enough at the pub or he doesn't even show up; he cancels dates for coffee, misses an appointment or forgets to write a recommendation letter for a former student, managing to get it in the mail a few days before the deadline date anyway.

He's always rushing to get somewhere or to get something done.

Frustrated, seeing his fatigue, I plead, "Just say no! You can say no."

And he'll reply, "I'll feel worse if I don't do it."

He's always rushing home to me. We know each other far too well to be able to hide some things. He knows how his presence soothes me. I know what a burden this can be to him.

Wolf is saying, It is what it is. Nothing less and nothing more.

~~~~

Ping! 3:00 a.m. I've slept for three hours and am now awake. Every morning the same, give or take a few minutes. I grab my blanket, pillow, headphones and Walkman and head for the living-room couch. Depositing everything, I return to the front hall, lift Finnegan up from her bed, and back in the living room place her gently down on the couch. She blinks groggily at me and goes back to sleep; she's used to this ritual now, too. Finnegan is my constant, loyal companion throughout this flare. I place the headphones over my ears, turn up the volume until every dark thought, every dark image is blasted out of my head by the music. I actually fall asleep during the second or third run-through of the tapes. I have my, "a night in san francisco" Van Morrison tape and "The Hunter" by Jennifer Warnes. This flare I add Phoebe Snow to the bill.

Listening to Jennifer Warnes's CD, I can hear the slightest intake of her breath, hear the last letter of a word as her tongue touches the roof of her mouth. It's the bass notes and her voice in "Way Down Deep" that act as an instant balm to my jangled nervous system.

I chatter to John and everyone else who drops by or calls during the day. My body is shaking and my mind's running fast. I'm baking, organizing my studio and the rest of the house. I'm eating everything in sight — especially sweets. I have thrush; my tongue feels dry and rough — like sandpaper. My mouth tastes swampy, how I imagine bog water would taste. My face is puffing up, becoming that weird, round, alien moon. An eye checkup reveals that two pinpoint cataracts — caused by high-steroid use and detected after my last flare — are a little bigger. My upper legs and arms lose their muscle tone. I'm weak and speedy at the same time, a seemingly impossible circumstance. The mustache, the hair falling out, the bruising, the interruption of my menstrual cycle, the weight loss, the weight gain. All the usual side effects.

But I'm different this time. I'm not afraid. I know the flare pattern. The medication is already working and this time I'm painting. For some reason I can concentrate, and sometimes, instead of listening to the music, I'll work quietly in my studio in the middle of the night.

There must be other people who are awake now too. Can't sleep for their own reasons. All I need now is a cigarette, a half-drunk bottle of scotch and a nude model to complete the romantic notion of a night in the life of an artist. I don't smoke or drink scotch. I could wake John for the nude model bit . . . but it is three in the morning; he might not be in the mood. I'll let him sleep.

The November exhibition is almost ready. *Free Spirit* is the last painting I do for the show and I paint it just a week before my exhibition opens.

Now, a year and a half after that flare, I look at this painting and am amazed. I painted it just as I began to reduce the prednisone. I knew I still had months and months of recovery to go, but it is the most optimistic painting, the most joyful painting of the whole series.

When I paint, I lose my self-consciousness, free to let the painting be what it wants to be. My experience is

220

sensory, not analytical. I'm drawn into a world free of everyday conflict. Losing myself in the act of painting, I can break away from the more mundane aspects of life, and most of all from the vagaries of disease. I'm grateful I paint, that I have the desire to brush paint over paper. The desire is the gift. It fuels and refuels my spirit, over and over again.

Picture this:

You are walking along a road overlooking Kalamalka Lake. You see a wind is causing a swell over the water. A child in a pink sweater runs behind a tree in a yard below you. You see orange poppies growing in gardens and clouds shifting light across surfaces. All of this information is stored in your memory — some of it consciously, some unconsciously. Later, you sit down to paint. This stored information reveals itself on paper as undulating lines, backlit shapes, pink swirls of colour surrounded by whirling forms: the child's joy. The air takes on weight, and is delicately fractured around a morning sun. Everything is alive and you can feel it.

This is your reality, your true experience of your walk above Kalamalka Lake.

~~~~

During this flare I am still very self-conscious about the way I look when I'm taking prednisone. The additional trauma of people seeing my face and body so distorted, as well as the usual one of showing my work, make me unsure if I want to attend the exhibition opening. I think about it on and off until one day I just think, *This is you. This is a part of your life. If you don't attend the opening, it will*

feel like someone else did those paintings. You'll miss that impor-
tant connection you feel when the work is finally on the walls and
your friends are there with you, drinking wine and celebrating.
I do go and it is a good thing to do.

Notes from my exhibition *The Language of Water* which was
held in Headbones Gallery in November of 1997:
"This summer, I swam half a mile in Kalamalka
Lake, as often as I could. I also sat at the edge of
the lake under willow trees, looking and finding
a microcosmic world in the water. I could see
minnows swimming just below the water's
surface and looking up, willow leaves turning in
the air above me. These small, similar shapes
seemed capable of a dual energy: minnows and
leaves flickering, quick one minute, still and
quiet the next. The white underbellies of the
minnows would glint as they darted here and
there; the silver undersides of the willow leaves
flashed in a similar way. And then stillness:
minnows resting in the cool dark water of the
willow's shade — willow leaves suspended,
branches trailing in the cool blue water.
In my head I expanded the vision into a bigger
landscape: the whole of the lake and the sky. I
imagined fish flying and leaves swimming in the
freedom of an ambiguous, 'open' world, a world
without compromise."

~~~~

Figure 11
If Fish Could Fly, 1997
Mixed Media

Figure 12
Water Spirit, 1997
Mixed media

Figure 13
Into the Winnowing Light, 1997
Mixed media

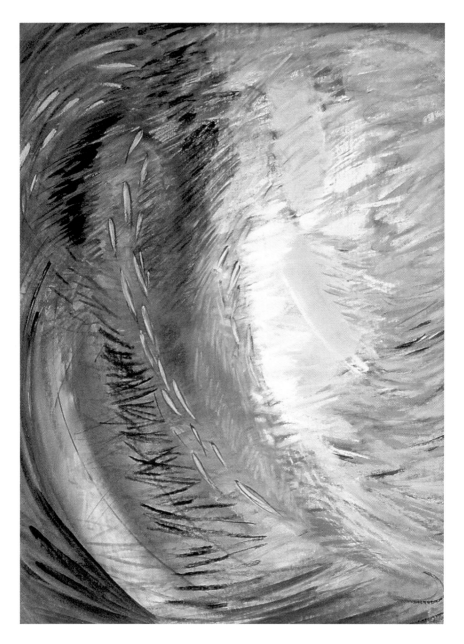

Figure 14
Night and Day, 1997
Mixed media

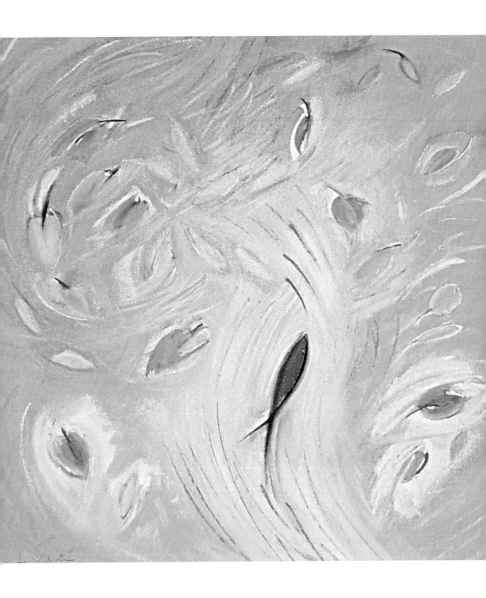

Figure 15
Free Spirit, 1997
Mixed media

Figure 16
Summerdance #1, 1999
Mixed media

I have a bone density test and after twenty-one years of non-stop steroid treatment (four high-dose periods, and in between an alternate day small maintenance dose) my test comes up normal. My bones are good. Very good. Even my doctors are impressed: "What have you been doing?"

"I take my calcium and vitamin D. I go for long walks and my family has good bones."

"Well, good for you!"

"Yes, good for me!"

~~~~

This time I am prepared for the inevitable fall into depression when the prednisone is reduced. I'm not willing to spend three or four months waiting for that to run its course. I know I don't need counselling. I need something pharmaceutical. My doctor suggests an anti-depressant and I gratefully try it and hope it will work. After several weeks, it begins to. I can't overestimate the relief. Now I begin the long process of building up my physical strength, of recovering from the double-drain (the drug therapy as well as the kidney disease) this flare has inflicted on my body and soul. I sleep and sleep. Gradually, two months later, my Achilles' tendons heal and I begin to take short walks around the neighbour-hood again. I begin to feel my "self" coming back.

I made it, once again. Remission. Wolf is sleeping and the fire, mere ash now.

May, 1998

"Here you go. Happy Anniversary, Jude!"

John hands me two tickets that say, Van Morrison, Joni Mitchel and Bob Dylan. In concert: GM Place, Vancouver.

I gasp, "You're kidding. Really?"

Grinning, "Really."

Gleefully, "Van Morrison!"

Joni Mitchel's album *Court and Spark* is the one John and I listened to, over and over again, years ago in Nelson, and Bob Dylan, well, he's just Bob Dylan, no explanation necessary.

Wrapping my arms around John, I whisper. "Thank you, thank you, thank you, my love."

Two weeks later, here we are, being led to our seats by the biggest, roughest-looking bouncer I've ever seen. It's impossible, but if we could be seen from where our friends Jeanne and Craig are sitting, we would be two specks way up, hundreds of rows up GM Place and off to the side, a bit behind the stage. Jeanne and Craig are at ground level, ten rows from centre stage, directly in front of the microphone Van Morrison will be singing into. Jeanne had called the ticket office a few days before the concert — it had been sold out for months — and the second before, someone had cancelled two tickets. Out of the blue, she got these two perfect seats.

Eyeing them through binoculars, I whine, "You'd think Jeanne and Craig would have given us those seats. They know how I feel about Van Morrison!" Jeanne and Craig are infamous for their generosity.

"I know," John agrees. "The bastards!"

Finally I see him (his back actually — a security guard on either side) walk up the stage stairs, over to the microphone. He puts his mouth to the harmonica, the band joins in, and he begins the first line of "The Burning Ground".

For the next two hours we are enchanted. Every once in awhile, Van Morrison turns and walks backstage for water. I hold the binoculars steady and for a minute glimpse his profile. Brian Kennedy is there too, and he makes a slow, complete turn once, face scanning the thousands of fans.

My cup runneth over.

~~~~

Sometime during this last flare, I finally have the epiphany I didn't know I was waiting to have.

Slow down. You're enough. What you do is enough. More than enough. Enough is enough. You won't turn back into that frightened, hesitant girl of so long ago. You're not that girl anymore. You can stop running.

The penny drops. I think I've got it.

~~~~

John and I talk it out. I make some decisions. I still want to teach, just not as much. So I resign from the Education Coordinator's job, continue going into the schools, but only two mornings a week. Occasionally I do professional development days for teachers and teach adult mixed-media art classes. I have a painting schedule that is less pressured; I paint now more than I ever did, but it's stretched out, more flexible, not packed into six weeks in the summer. I'm enjoying a daily life that can meander, be flexible and change depending on my energy.

For the first time in years I feel an absence of urgency, of pressure in my life from myself. I always felt like I had to hurry in order to get everything done before the disease flared again. I've let myself slow down. Actually, my life feels like it did those two wonderful years away in France and Scotland, when I left Wolf and my worries and self-criticism behind in Canada. It's so good to feel this at home, in my own house, in this day-to-day life with John.

Did I need to push so hard? Did I need to accomplish all that I did? No. But, in the end, this pushing is what brought me to the place I'm in now. I know truly, deeply, what I've been through, who and what I am. I have come to know the breadth of my own resolve and my natural capacity for joy. This knowledge is irrevocable, something that is my own, gained through the experience of living with lupus. I am quietly confident this knowledge will help to sustain me through whatever the lupus holds for me in the future.

Having said all this, I imagine a future kidney flare buoyed by all that I have learned. Is it clear sailing? *Of course not.* At the mere thought of a flare, my response is physical, a contraction in the gut and an emptying of the heart. All this newfound wisdom flies out the window in the face of the actual event. But I know now there is something beyond that initial response, something deep within me that will carry me through.

Yes.

I feel strong and well. In remission. Between kidney flares, aside from the fatigue, I'm asymptomatic. I start the day off with a walk or go to the gym and do light weight exercises. Very light. I'm not interested in sweating, just making my body stronger. My muscles love the feel of the weights. I haven't had any arthritic pain for years. Occasionally my chest will ache right through to my back when the weather changes, or strangely, when I'm menstruating, but it never develops into anything. I just lie down on a heating pad with my head and torso raised.

I've done well as far as the renal involvement is concerned. My kidneys still function without the aid of dialysis. Even dialysis doesn't terrify me the way it did when I first learned I had kidney disease. I've been told kidney transplants are highly successful in lupus patients, and that the disease has even been known to dissipate afterwards. I'm older now, calmer, less afraid. I have the wisdom of experience, of long experience managing this disease. I've made it past that antiquated Merck Manual prognosis that so haunted me even after I was told it was outdated. The prognosis for lupus patients is now good, especially if diagnosed early and if the patient listens to what their body tells them.

I've had four kidney flares: the initial one, after a scorching, unprotected summer when I didn't know yet I was photosensitive. The second, after my appendix was removed. The third, when I decreased the immunosuppressive azathioprine too much, and the last one at the end of a particularly hot summer. I know it is likely there will be more. I have no idea when or how bad they'll be or how long I'll be able to function without dialysis. This doesn't seem to be the issue right now. The important thing is that right now, today, I feel well and happy and strong.

I can't say the thought of more steroid therapy doesn't upset me. It does. I dread it. Cyclophosphimide is now the recommended drug therapy for kidney disease that is caused by the overall immune disorder of systemic lupus.

If I could have anything at all — short of a total cure — it would be to be rid of the fatigue of lupus. For me, the fatigue is still the most discouraging manifestation of the disease, still the most relentless and frustrating aspect to manage. It can overwhelm me, usually when my rest schedule has been altered and I've reached that, *I'm too tired to undress for bed, too tired to utter a word* stage. Even in remission, the fatigue is there. I've had to accept the reality that no amount of sleep or careful management of my energy can ever completely relieve its presence. I fantasize about one entire day without feeling the weight of this exhaustion, one entire day without carefully planning each activity around my energy, the same way some people dream about winning the lottery. How that would feel. How I would spend my energy. Who I could share it with.

Until the cure for lupus is found, this is just that, a fantasy. In the meantime, I've developed a daily routine that helps. My fatigue follows a fairly consistent pattern. I'm at my best early in the morning. Around one or two in the afternoon I start to flag. I sleep for a couple of hours and can now fall asleep in minutes. I look forward to this sleep because it's what my body needs and I've finally seen and accepted that. Everything about my life is easier when I follow this daily routine — easier for me *and* for the people around me. I now wake from a nap refreshed and seldom wake tired in the mornings. I know I can alter this fatigue to a degree. That at least is in my power.

I do know, still, what normal tiredness feels like. I feel it: after I've been out tramping around Kal Park with John and Finnegan, or raking leaves in our yard in the fall, or planting annuals in the spring — this kind of tiredness, I can easily live with. After these kinds of activities, my muscles feel the healthy ache of physical activity and my mind feels yawn-tired not cell-exhausted. Normal tiredness is luxury tiredness to me. Even though I have tried to describe the fatigue of lupus, all my words fall short. You couldn't know what it feels like unless you had it.

There are things that I still long for. I long to swim to the farthest yellow buoy in the middle of a brilliant, sunny day, when the water is aqua-green and diamonds are sparkling off its surface. I long to walk out into the sun without fear, tipping my face to its rays, as I once did as a child. To feel the simple, free joy of that.

Every three months I do my blood and kidney-function tests. Each time, I wonder and hope everything is OK. If something unusual happens in my body, such as an intestinal infection, or shingles or even if I cut my hand, I wonder if it will trigger a flare. There will always be this anxiety. The difference now is that I have acquired a healthier perspective, the skills to cope, and more knowledge to draw on.

I remember sitting in a doctor's office when I was twenty-three years old — about six months after I'd been told I'd developed kidney disease — saying impatiently, "I just think I should be able to accept this and get on with my life. But I keep falling apart." And the doctor saying, "You will be coping with this for the rest of your life." My heart emptied as it always does when I'm really afraid and I wanted to scream, "Don't say that!" But I didn't. I went outside to my car and sobbed until I thought I'd never stop. It was the worst possible thing that could have been said to me. I was twenty-three years old. I had a whole lifetime ahead of me and I had interpreted his sure words as cold confirmation that I was destined to a life of continual pain and fear.

Now, from an older and more experienced perspective, I know that his words were true. But my twenty-three-year-old self could not bear to hear what sounded like a life to be lived in purgatory. *Caution, good doctors. Caution.*

~~~~

John and I have a repertoire of lupus in-jokes, like pleading fatigue when trying to get out of a boring or unpleasant task.

"Oh no, I'm sorry, I won't be able to do that. I have lupus, you know."

And John's response, "Unfortunately, I won't be able to do it either. I *live* with someone who has lupus, you know."

~~~~

It's here I want to state the obvious. John lives with this disease too. It's been important for him to have a neutral place to let down. He copes with lupus from the "well" person's perspective and has a whole raft of his own responses to the demands of that. There have been times when he has wanted a private, objective point of view from a professional who could listen to him without being hurt, responding with guilt, or misunderstanding what he's trying to say. He has his own story to tell.

I realized a long time ago that the kind of support I sometimes asked of John or my sister, Franny, simply by speaking my fears out loud, was too great. *They* couldn't make the disease go away, and to keep voicing my anxieties to them after a certain point was unfair, exhausting, and scary for *them*. Also, these anxieties, though very real at the time, could be fleeting; just the dawn of a new day could put them in a better perspective. I've learned to wait for them to pass, knowing that they *will* pass.

There are now lupus support groups everywhere in the world. They've been formed by patients who long to talk to other people who will understand exactly how they're feeling, people who'll know the full ramifications of having and living with lupus. These groups invite professionals such as pharmacists, doctors, and psychologists to their meetings, people who have specific information pertinent to lupus and general information, too, that's helpful to anyone living with a chronic disease.

I remember the first time I attended a support meeting. It was the first one ever in our town, instigated by another woman who has lupus. There were only six people in attendance but their impact on me was enormous. I was sitting, for the first time ever, in the company of people who *knew*. I listened to the others' stories and learned very quickly why lupus is called "the disease with a thousand faces". No two women had the same physical manifestations, but we were all struggling with the same emotional demands of living day to day with this disease. There was lots of laughter, helpful advice and practical information passed around. It was good medicine.

Chronic disease is different from acute illness. The difference is that very often an acute illness has a cure, or at least the possibility of a cure, and a chronic disease like lupus doesn't. Yet. People talk about *battling* an acute illness and very often, with the right medical treatment and, it seems, pure willpower and a positive attitude, they're successful. The disease is cured or goes into remission, never to return.

At the beginning, I looked at lupus first as something to run from, and then as something to battle. I do neither now. The medications do the battling for me. Having an autoimmune disease means that there already is a battle going on inside me — my body is at war with itself. Thinking I could and then actually trying to control the disease just made me more tired and, at times, even more sick. Fighting it made me unable to face the changes I needed to make in my everyday life in order to become as healthy as I could be. Fighting it delayed my acceptance of the disease. It was learning how to live *with* the disease that has brought me the acceptance and the kind of peace and even health I have now.

I don't ever want to underestimate the daily struggle of having a disease like lupus. It's very hard. There are people who suffer more and people who suffer less than I do. No two are alike. Each person has his or her own story to tell. The writer Flannery O'Connor had lupus. So did Ferdinand Marcos, past President of the Philippines. Past President George Bush's *dog* had lupus. There are five people who have the disease — I hope this is a freakishly abnormal number — living within a two-block radius of my house. *It's a natural instinct for wolves to form a pack, isn't it?* I don't think lupus is any more prevalent than it used to be. I just think it's more easily diagnosed. I suspect people with mild cases used to live their entire lives without ever knowing what was wrong with them.

Spring, 1998

I begin brushing a few random strokes of Sap green lengthwise down the paper. The light is just right at 9:00

a.m. through my studio window and John is working, too, writing at the other end of the house.

John always writes listening to jazz. This morning, the sounds of Pat Metheny fill the house. John's office is a sunroom off the living room, a room bright with natural light from the two large windows that fill two walls of the room. His computer sits on a desk he designed and built himself, between these two windows. The third wall is lined with shelves that are filled, floor to ceiling, with books and periodicals. The fourth wall, the entranceway, has French doors and a window on either side which I've covered with lined rattan blinds to give him more privacy.

John has fixed up this room in the same way he's fixed up all of his writing rooms since we met. The walls are papered with posters, photographs of friends and family (roughly half of our twenty-one nieces and nephews are represented), postcards, memos and lists of writing projects. A piece of green jade sits between him and the computer. An artist had cut and polished it especially for him from the memorial stone she'd been commissioned to carve for a friend of John's who had died. She knew how much Jack had meant to John. There are several other talismans from other friends arranged on the window ledges. Propped up against the paper holder is a postcard of one of Derain's paintings, a brilliant blue and orange landscape, and a photograph of John and I taken in France.

If I walked into the kitchen right now, I'd be able to see John tapping the keyboard of his computer, lost in whatever it is he's writing. He's probably working on a short story. There is, no doubt, a cup of coffee at his elbow. I know all is well with John when he's in his office writing.

He's been in his office writing a lot this spring.

I pick up a black conte crayon and make a broad, curved line over the paper. Dip a paintbrush in aurilean yellow, and smudge a wavy line next to the black one. Brush clear water in a loose, large rectangle over a corner of the paper. Drop a bit of alizarin red into the wet. Watch the red dissipate to a tint. *There now. A warm glow. Nothing too fiery.*

August 1998

The second the sun drops behind the hill, Alison shrieks, "We can go now!" She and I swim out to the second yellow buoy. It's the farthest she's ever gone (Alison is seven years old) and she is delighted. After our mandatory circling and touching of the buoy, we head back to shore. We're both on our backs, kicking up great splashes of white foam, gazing up at the sky and watching the clouds shifting shape.

Alison exclaims, "I see a face! I see an ice cream cone!"

I glance over and see her, a small bundle in an orange lifejacket, tanned legs kicking furiously, eyes wide open to the cerulean sky.

She says seriously, "Auntie Jude? I wish you weren't allergic to the sun. It feels so nice on my face. I wish you were allergic to carrots instead." She knows I hate carrots.

We laugh, turn over in the water and wave at the rest of the family back on shore.

Early September, 1998

I get up at 6:00 a.m., before the sun rises over Middleton Mountain. I put on my bathing suit, open and close the door quietly. John is still sleeping. I walk across the grass to the end of the pier and sit down.

It's then I notice Wolf sitting facing me across the water, on the neighbour's pier. We look with curiosity at one another. For the first time, I sense no malevolence in him. For the first time, Wolf senses no fear in me.

I can accept his periodic intrusions into my life if he can accept that for long periods of time I won't even think about him. That I can and will live my life without anticipating the feel of his hot breath on my neck or the sound of his tread in the night. We nod. It's agreed then.

I lower myself into the water, swim to the first yellow buoy, circle round, and swim back to the pier just as the morning sun begins to fracture the water, the trees and hills, the sky, into angular prisms of light. Cezanne is here, in the valley, this morning.

I see Wolf turn, trot down the pier and into the brush. I look up and see John through the cabin window. He walks from the bedroom into the kitchen and over to the sink. I know he's filling the coffeepot with water and the filter with coffee. I know he's taking two pottery mugs from the cupboard and placing them on the old fir table.

I know Finnegan is still asleep, on top of the bed by now, in the other room.

John turns as I open the cabin door. I stand there dripping water on the linoleum floor and we grin at one another.

"Good Morning."

"Good Morning."

Figure 17
Water Garden, 2001
Mixed media

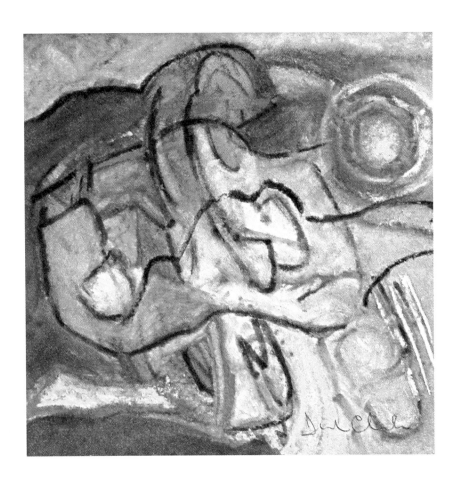

Figure 18
Moonglow, 2001
Mixed Media

February, 2000

"I'd like to meet that little boy."

Throughout the weekend, John and I watch the progress of Variety Club's Show of Hearts Telethon on BCTV. The donations keep building, the hosts, entertainers and volunteers taking the calls are upbeat, galvanized by the generosity of the public.

Short documentaries portraying the lives of several selected children are repeated intermittently throughout the fundraiser. One story especially moves me. It's about a boy named Christopher who's seven. He has juvenile rheumatoid arthritis and I can tell by the roundness of his face that he's taking steroids. He sits on his mother's lap, looking at her and listening intently as she talks about the pain he's been suffering since he was two. She explains that she couldn't hold or even touch him for a long time because it hurt him too much. Then she looks down at him, smiles tenderly, and says, "You know all about this, don't you?" Christopher solemnly nods his head.

A few days later I'm visiting a friend and tell her about Christopher. She says, "I think that's the boy they profiled in the Vernon paper a couple of weeks ago. I think he lives in Lumby or Lavington."

Christopher attends school just fifteen minutes away from our house.

I call the school and talk to his teacher, explain why I'd like to meet Christopher and ask if I could come to the school so he and I can do some drawing and painting together.

The teacher is enthusiastic and we arrange a time and date for the following week.

~~~~

The third time I arrive at the school, Christopher greets me excitedly. "I'm going to the gym today! Look! They got me this machine. You can come and watch me if you want!" Christopher makes it quite clear there will be no art today. He's got things to do, people to meet, places to go.

"I would love to watch you, Christopher."

"Here, put me in!"

"Oh, no. I don't think so. I don't know how to move you and I don't want to hurt you."

He states with authority, "It's easy. You just hold me here, and here, and then lift."

"No, Christopher, I want to wait for your teacher."

"OK," he says, in a tone of patience far beyond his years.

~~~~

Now we are in the gym. The walker supports Christopher's weight so his feet can rest easily when he's not moving, and when he wants to take off a light push on his tippy-toes propels him forward. The wheels of Christopher's walker spin over the gymnasium floor. He's weightless. He's flying. He circles and runs away from and catches the other children, criss-crossing the room, again and again. His giggles echo through the air; the other children join in, delighted, too, with his freedom.

April, 2000

There's something else waiting around the corner for me. Something bigger and more mysterious than what I had found and come to understand during my last kidney flare in 1997.

Something magical.

~~~~

Wolf finds me unafraid and living a happy, healthy life.

It starts out innocently enough with a call from my GP, Dr. Lindsay's, office. "Hi Jude, it's Janine. Nothing to worry about. Lauren just wants you to see her or Dr. Bouma to discuss your latest lab tests."

I have my three-month checkup on Monday with Dr. Bouma and he'll have the results. I decide to wait and see him. When I put the phone down, I'm not concerned. *She said nothing to worry about.* So I forget about it and continue planning my sister's birthday party which is two weeks away.

April 3

"It looks like the lupus is active, Jude. The lab tests indicate your kidney function is being affected. Do the tests again, and I'll call Dr. Penn. Come back and see me in a week. Then we'll see what to do."

My heart empties. I look away from Dr. Bouma and at a calendar on the wall. Above the date schedule is a photograph of a lion lying in tall grass in the wild. *It must be South Africa. That's where he's from.*

April 11

John and I sit down across from Dr. Bouma. He says immediately, "Dr. Penn said, 'Let's not get too excited just yet.' I'd like you to do the tests again, Jude, and then we'll see."

I flash John a "lighted up" look. He doesn't return it.

But now I'm convinced I'm *not* flaring. I feel too well. It's the wrong time of year — spring, not the end of summer. It's three or even five years too soon — not my flare pattern at all. I am confident telling my family and friends, "Nope, there's been a mistake. I'm not flaring." This isn't false hopefulness. I believe it.

May 2

Diane calls from Dr. Bouma's office. "He'd like you to come in to discuss your tests. Can you come tomorrow?"
I'm flaring.
I won't be able to go to Yellowknife now.

May 3

Dr. Bouma's office is large with a big window. I stood at the window one day and pointed out the roof of John's and my house across town to him.

Today Dr. Bouma and I are sitting across from each other at his desk. He says with sympathy, "I know you don't want to go on the high doses of steroids."

I reply resignedly, "And I know I have to. It's my miracle drug. It's always worked before."

Then my voice becomes fierce, "But this flare is just *impossible.*"

He looks at me with interest, "Why?"

"Because I *don't* flare in the spring and it's too soon after the last one. The flares have been going seven years, another seven years, then five, and now this one, a year and a half from the last. I'm worried about how close this flare is to the last one. Will this be the pattern now? Could it just be an aberration? With me, there's usually a cause. I haven't figured it out yet."

May 5

My sister and I are seated across from one another at the table in our living room. I say bitterly, "All my life, I've been sucking the life out of everyone I love."

"No, no. Don't say that. You haven't been."

"Yes, I have. Ever since I was a little girl, needing constant reassurance, consoling, being told I'm doing a good job. And then John. He's had to live this disease with me. I can't bear to think of him having to go through another flare. It's the last week of classes. It's his summer break. It's too soon for a flare. I don't flare in the summer. And Mom's got such a bad cold. I haven't been able to go in and keep her company. I pass meals through the door. Call her on the phone."

"I know that's been bothering you."

"Bothering me! It makes me feel useless. Completely useless. And here I am, right now, laying this on you. Demanding attention again, this way. I'm doing it right now."

May 13

John is scheduled to go to the Leighton Artist Colony at the Banff Centre with Neil, the Fraser of the Lent/Fraser/Wall Trio. They're to have their own studio in the woods of the Rocky Mountains. They'll be surrounded by trees, have peace and quiet, and the odd cranky elk to amuse them. Neil and John have had this planned for months and are excited about having the time to focus on some new songs.

I want him to go. I'll be fine and he needs this break.

But for two weeks now my nervous system has been reacting to the high doses of prednisone in its usual way. I can't rest during the day and have fitful half-hour sleeps here and there during the night. By five in the afternoon the day before John is to leave for Banff I'm desperate, sitting in tears on the window seat in my studio. I don't think I can get through one more day like this, let alone a week with John away. I'm so wound up I can't sit still. My brain has been running at top speed for a week. *I'm ragged, desperate to get some sleep.*

And *voila!* I make a smart decision. I call Dr. Lindsay's office and catch her just before she's leaving. For the first time in all these years I tell a doctor exactly how I'm feeling. I don't try to make it sound inconsequential, or like something I should be able to take care of myself. Dr. Lindsay tells me she'll call a prescription in to the pharmacy and that I should take the sedative a half hour before I want to sleep. And then she says, "Don't try to do this all on your own, Jude. You can't do this by yourself."

I hang up the phone and burst into tears. "That's all I had to do all these years. It was so easy to do that. To ask for something to help me sleep."

John looks at me in dismay. "I didn't even know how hard that was for you. You need to sleep. I'm going to go and get the prescription right away." He stands up and leaves the room.

Do you think that you should be able to will yourself to sleep? You take medications that contain powerful chemicals which cause insomnia. And you question the integrity of taking a pill that will help alleviate that? Is it only Wolf who torments? Aren't you doing a pretty good job of that yourself? Again?

A short time later John returns and hands me the prescription bottle. I place a pill under my tongue and twenty minutes later I'm asleep on the couch.

From now on I can sleep during the day. I sleep through the night until four or five in the morning. Since I don't need Van, Jennifer or Phoebe in the middle of the night, I listen to them as I'm falling asleep in the afternoon.

It took me twenty years to make that phone call: five kidney flares, months of sleepless, jangled days and nights.

May 14th

Neil arrives early. We joke and laugh and I tease John and him about being good in Banff. I remind them they should hope Julia and I are, too, back here at home.

Towards the end of the week, I call Dr. Bouma to get the results of my second blood and urine tests. The serum creatinine has come down a bit and there is just a trace of protein in my urine. The drugs are already working.

I phone the Banff Centre. "Hi, *c'est moi.*"

"Hi, *moi!* How are you?"

"I'm great and I've got good news."

"Are you really OK? You're not hiding anything from me, are you?"

"No, in fact I'm trying to keep a lid on things. Something's happening to me this time. Something really good. I don't know what it is and I've only been feeling it for a couple of days so . . . I'll try to explain it to you when you get home. How are *you* doing?"

"Great. We're working hard. I feel just as spoiled as ever being here."

May 20th

John's home from Banff. We're sitting across from each other on the couches in the living room, telling each other about our week apart. I say, "It began as a physical sensation. I could feel the tension as an actual weight leaving my body. Muscle by muscle. Each day I felt a little lighter. Then it felt as if my heart was beginning to relax, beat a slower rhythm. I could be feeling quite speedy from the prednisone and all I had to do was lie down on the couch and centre myself. I did it with my mind. I'd feel completely relaxed within minutes. And for two weeks now, my mood has stayed buoyant. I know the prednisone does that to me, but this feels different. It's a calm, steady kind of buoyancy. Not a hyper kind. I don't know what this is but I'm just going to enjoy it. It doesn't matter if it's only the prednisone. Its happening and I feel great."

Over the next three weeks I find myself going about my days in a state of calm elation. I wake in the morning alert and energized. I write for a couple of hours, then make a pot of coffee and wake John.

~~~~

We paint the patio grey-green, and I place two blue glazed pots brimming with yellow nasturtiums and blue lobelias in the corner by the shed. I intermingle three different clematises, attach them to trellises against the shed and tie string along the bottom of the side fence so the ivy can crawl along it. We buy four blue and white-striped lawn chairs, arrange them around a table under the dense shade of the Manitoba Maple and Chestnut trees, and place a new rattan mat at the entrance to the kitchen door.

One of John's brothers, Frankie, and his wife, Debbie, and their three kids moved to Vernon five years ago. Debbie keeps us stocked with home-baked goodies, bringing them by or having us up to their house a couple of times a week.

One of their children, Vanessa, is taking creative writing from John, and during term they commute together to and from Kelowna. John and I have seventeen nieces and nephews on his side, all living in Edmonton, and it just so happens that the one who moved to Vernon decided to go into Honours English and Creative Writing. It happened because Vanessa, after she'd completed a year, decided to take a semester off, unsure if she wanted to continue in the Anthropology program. John suggested she audit one of his creative writing classes, just for something to do. She fell in love with literature and language. And the rest is history, as they say.

~~~~

I bake muffins or ginger cake early every morning and invite friends who don't have to go to work over for coffee. I bring out the blue tablecloth I bought in France and set the outside table with pottery dishes, fruit salads, cheeses, and the baked goodies. My friends and I have warm, close visits and laugh a lot.

Lana pokes her head around the fence one morning and I ask her back for coffee after she walks the youngest of her four sons, Cameron, to school.

She says, "Jude, you've created your own little paradise here! Its looks very French."

I beam at her.

~~~~

Whenever the idea enters my head that all of this could be unreal, that it's just the prednisone, I remind myself, *So what if it is? It doesn't matter. It's as real as anything is. Don't analyze it.* And when I feel so grateful for all of this, so surprised at it all, I think, too, *Why not all of this? Why shouldn't I have this?* In fact, "why not" becomes my mantra.

Nothing bothers me. I have clear, concise solutions to any problem anyone else might have. I become, as usual while I'm taking high doses of prednisone, the home-maker I've never been. Our home is spick and span. I don't start organizing cupboards and drawers this flare, but my friend Linda suggests I start a home business: "People could drop their 'junk drawers' off at your place on their way to work in the morning and then pick them up, all meticulously reorganized, on their way home. You could make some money off this flare, Jude!"

Warming to the idea I add, "I could offer them advice, too. Counsel them about their problems, figure out their lives for them while I'm at it. You know how *smart* I am when I'm on prednisone."

"Yeah," Linda says. "That would double your income! And think how grateful everyone would be. Now that's what I'd call a great job."

I've let go of a heaviness that's been weighing me down all these years. This isn't such a huge revelation. People are doing this all over the world every day. Recovering from something. Finally understanding something about themselves or their situation and finding a way to feel better, to make it better. What *is* huge for me is that I thought I'd reached the farthest point of self-knowledge, peace and understanding in the last flare, in 1997.

And now this is happening. The forest is thinning, the world becoming a lighter place, still. The wolf senses it first. Then she sees it through the branches: a small triangle of cyan. There, now. The lake. It has never looked a more hopeful blue.

My head feels clear. Ideas for paintings come easily. Ideas have always had to share space in my head with all that other clutter. It's been a tight fit. Now the images are flowing smoothly.

May 24th

I'm sitting in the reception room of the hospital lab, waiting to have some tests done. It's early, eight in the morning, and since it's Saturday there aren't any other patients here. I had to make special arrangements. It's just me and a fish tank. I'm watching the fish darting here and there and soon have an *aha!* moment. *I know. I'll make up an image to use on that clutter in case it ever reappears.*

I visualize my childhood nightmare. In my head, I alter all the tangled ropes into one thin, light strand and tie it securely to a clump of my hair. I imagine myself walking into Kalamalka Lake, pushing off into the water at waist level and swimming towards the first yellow buoy. Streaming behind me, the strand flickers, glints in a gentle, iridescent light.

May 26th

It's early evening. I've been "surveying the ponderosa", dead-heading as I walk around the garden. I find John on the patio tuning his guitar and Finnegan stretched out at his feet. John puts the guitar down while Finnegan bounds over and pushes her nose into the bucket of flower heads beside me.

Something I had written about in the morning had stayed with me all day. I want to tell John about it.

"I just wrote about going with Mom to visit Dad in the hospital, after he'd had shock treatment. I was about ten and I remember walking into his room. He was lying on this metal hospital bed and — "

"Oh . . . ," John stands up and comes over to me. "You don't have to — "

"No. No, this is good. This is all right."

My voice is low, anguished, and tears flood my cheeks: "He was so sick. And there was nothing we could do to help him."

John says gently, "You loved him so much, Jude. He knew that."

~~~~

My tests continue to show improvement.

May 29th

We're having coffee on the patio after dinner. John has to leave in a few minutes for a gig in Armstrong.

I say excitedly, "I've figured out what it is. It's fear. It's fear leaving my body. It's like there's been some kind of dense mass stuck in there and it's finally getting unstuck and moving out. I thought that at the end of the last flare that I'd made my peace with the disease. I'd accepted it, and was feeling just about as good as I could possibly feel. I wrote that vignette about Wolf and I looking at each other on the pier at the lake. I was conscious of being unafraid then. Wolf and I *had* made our peace with one another. All this is true. Mentally, it had happened. You know, our life had changed again, opened up even more for you and I."

John nods his head but doesn't say anything.

"But now I realize something was still there, an actual form with weight. It was less heavy than before, but still there. It's left my body now, too."

I can't tell what John's thinking. *He's probably thinking this is the prednisone talking.*

His reticence doesn't dissuade me, "When I was told I was flaring again this time, I thought Wolf *had* betrayed me. He had shown up in the form of another kidney flare, but these past few weeks I've been looking around for him, expecting him to be more . . . *present.* You know — that darker shadow hanging over me when the disease is flaring. But I'd begun to look at Wolf as a kind of benevolent watchdog. It seemed his purpose now was to warn me when something was coming my way. Caution me to take more care. Now it seems like he's done that and he's backed away. He's just not here."

Quietly, "I'm doing this on my own, now. Wolf's left me on my own."

"It's like that time when I was bouncing the ball on the slate path when I was nine years old and feeling like I had something to do with making my headache disappear. *I've* done this. *I've* had the power to change how I see the disease and how it affects my life."

John still doesn't say anything. He's leaning back in his lawn chair, one hand stroking Finnegan's head, listening.

"When I was diagnosed with lupus at twenty-one, I figured it out in my head. I would die at forty-three. Unless some other acute critical lupus attack got me before. I have no idea how I came up with that age but it's been sitting there in my heart for twenty-four years."

I pause and then say wonderingly, "And now it's gone. I never thought I'd get this. I never thought I'd get this, too."

John's eyes finally tell me.

The scraping sound of metal on pavement suddenly breaks the quiet and Finnegan races, barking, to the fence. She's doing her best teeth-bared, Tasmanian Devil, guard dog impression, informing the boy flying by on his skateboard just exactly who's boss.

~~~~

I started writing this book when I was forty-three.

May 30th

It's five in the morning and I'm up writing. Outside my window the lawns are bright with spring green. The day is soft and benevolent. There's a little mist, a drizzle in the air. Sun's still sleeping. So is John. Finnegan's right beside him. On *top* of the down duvet, of course.

Whoosh! There goes the last vestige of Fear. Out of my body and out the open window. Fear must weigh a ton. Sorrow lifts and takes a little greyness with her. Anger is thinning out, becoming healthy, in spite of herself. Now Grudge. Whoosh! There goes another hundred pounds. Grudge has always been a pain in the butt. Self-criticism. Now her I send off with tender loving care, and a reminder to myself to always look out for her. She may need extra attention now and then. Vanity's reluctant to leave so I give her a little shove. She's a pest, that one. She'll be back, for sure. In fact, they'll all return from time to time.

Whew! I'm buoyant. I'm so light now; I'm a leaf floating on air. I'm Scrooge on Christmas day, hanging out the window, realizing he hasn't missed the party after all.

Now who's that wafting in through the open window? It's Smell, bringing the fragrance of lilac with her. Mirth is floating in, too. Irony's with her. Irony always adds a little drama, a little zip. Peace is floating on water. Joy is touching everything and everyone with loving hands. Colour is every fine tint, every boldness it wants to be. Taste is cream, a piece of heaven sliding down my throat. Sound is sharp, then soft — adagio.

Touch is an old hand-knit green woolen sweater of my father's.

Love has always been here. She's an old friend and I'm grateful for her sureness, her ease, her generosity. She doesn't ask for anything — she just is.

And Health. Health is here now, too. Health has had the hardest task of all. So much has been demanded of her. She's come through the darkest nights with dignity. She's a hero, health is. She's been here before, for long periods of time, years, but I'm never sure how long she'll stay; I never know when she's going to leave or how long it'll be before she's back again. I try to understand the unpredictable nature of her personality. When and how

she arrives is, in the end, her own decision. I'm celebrating her now. Making her feel welcome.

This is lupus. This is morning-time. This is life.

May

There are white peonies blooming everywhere this week.
B.B. King has changed the lyrics to the song. He's
singing, "The Thrill [Ain't] Gone". Even Van Morrison
is happy. He's singing, "Mama Told Me There'd Be Days
Like This".

~~~~

Virginia's two stories place first and third in the short story
competition. Franny asserts herself and doesn't get an
office with a window but does get her chair back. Mom
gets a birdie at golf. Dave Arnason tells Louise that her
writing is "delightful, excellent really". John's newly
published chapbooks of poems, *Black Horses, Cobalt Suns*,
arrives in the mail. I count fourteen golden-yellow buds
on my Hibiscus plant. Lana completes her teaching
diploma and gets her first call to substitute teach. Sharon
plans a trip to England and Scotland this summer with
our young nieces, Sarah and Alison. John's sister, Susan,
requests a transfer to another school and it's granted;
she'll teach her last two years before retirement in a brick,
vine-covered school close to where she grew up.

Rita gives birth to her and Mark's beautiful baby boy.

*I think I'll go out and buy a red T-shirt today. And wear it,
too.*

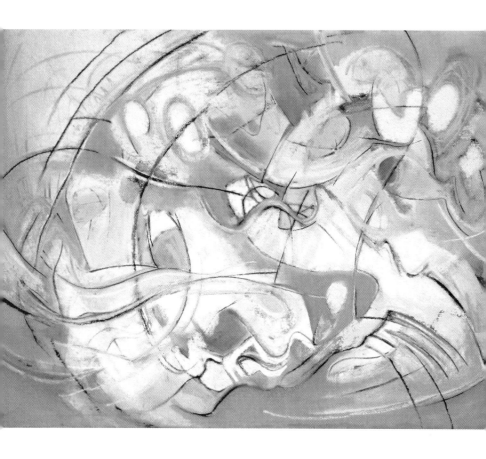

Figure 19
Grace, 2001
Mixed media

June 1st to 6th

All week long, the days are cool and misty. Occasional sun-breaks make the grass, shrubs, sidewalks and streets glisten with freshness. One day I dash from my car through the delicate sunlight to enter a mall, and when I return to leave a while later, find a dark sky, a torrent of rain beating a steady, strong rhythm against the ground. People are racing for their cars, cars' windshield wipers are jerking back and forth, ineffectual against the sudden downpour.

I go out into it, raise my face to the sky and feel a benediction.

June 5th

I call the elementary school to explain why I haven't been out to see Christopher for the last few weeks and ask how he's doing.

The secretary tells me he's in hospital. "He's been in the hospital for three weeks." I want to ask her why but refrain. She isn't at liberty to give me that kind of information. I could call his mother. But I've only met her once. It would be an intrusion. I'll wait a couple of weeks and then call the school again.

June 7th

Mom holds the door open and I walk carefully past her down the stairs carrying a tray with two tall glasses of iced tea. Reaching the bottom safely, I walk around the corner of her house and over to the shadiest area of the back garden. Mom pulls the lawn chairs in closer to a small table and we settle in. Lately, we've been discussing my father and his illness. She's become used to my questions, and today I want to ask her about something that she said to me a long time ago.

I pick up my glass of iced tea and hold it against my cheek. "Mom, you told me once that you never talked to your parents about Dad's illness."

She says offhandedly, "Well, I think they knew something was wrong but we never actually discussed it." Pointing to a planter nearby, she exclaims, "Look at those begonias! Aren't they beautiful?"

"They sure are. But how did you cope? Was there a place in your head you could go to for comfort, for relief?"

"If I was alone, I'd go downstairs to Franny's room and just try and empty my head of all of it. Or have a really good cry."

"Did you pray?"

She looks at me earnestly. "Oh yes, I've always prayed. Not in an organized religion kind of way. I didn't know who or what I was praying to. It was just something I believed in, a presence or a spirit or something and it gave me great comfort. You better move your chair, dear. The sun's catching your arm."

I comply and shift my chair. I reach over and pick up the sunscreen tube on the table, slather my arms and face, and pull my visor down a little lower. My face is still tingling — *it's just the heat,* and carry on: "So what then? You came back upstairs and everything was OK again?'

Mom's eyes widen and she says emphatically, "No, Jude, it wasn't OK again. It was hell. And as time went by, it became harder and harder for me. And then your Dad was finally put on lithium and our life together changed."

"So when did you hit the wall? What was your worst moment?"

"After your father died. That's when it all hit me. You know that. I would end up on your doorstep at six in the morning. I'd have been awake all night, full of anxiety and fear."

I say slowly, wonderingly, "That was the first time that you had ever shown me your vulnerability and let *me* support *you.*"

"I suppose." She doesn't say anything for a minute, and then, "That was when I needed your father the most. After he died." She smiles at the irony of what she's just said. "I'd look at that photograph of him — the one taken out at the cabin the day after Franny and Don's wedding — and say, "You should be here helping me through this. It's your turn."

I sigh, dismayed. "You spent most of your married life coping with Dad's illness, and then when he finally got well, I got sick. You've always dealt with illness, not as the one who is sick but as the support person."

"Yes," she agrees, managing to put indignation, resignation and sorrow, in that one small word.

I add guiltily, "John and I leaned so heavily on you when we moved back to Vernon."

She reaches out and bats at a fly sitting on the rim of her glass. "Scram!" She admits, "It was hard. I'd see you drive up the driveway and wonder right off what kind of day you were having. You'd come in all bouncy and smiling. You'd manage to keep that up for about five minutes and then you'd just dissolve into tears. It was hard to bear that, hard for a mother to bear. I used to wonder if I had done something wrong during my pregnancy to cause your illness."

"Well, you know Dr. Bouma nixed that worry, emphatically."

"Yes."

Brushing my hair off my forehead, I roll my eyes and groan, " I was such a little pain in the butt when I was a kid. Worry, worry, worry. You listened to me — you've always listened to me. I've thought about this a lot and when I think of what you were coping with yourself . . . "

She says simply, "I wouldn't have had it any other way, honey."

Looking around her garden, I ask, "Do you want a piece of my pincushion plant? Mine's big enough to split. It's a really pretty shade of blue and it's hardy, too. The stems are so strong the sprinkler doesn't beat them down."

"Sure. I've got just the spot for it."

"So! Are you all packed and ready to go?"

"I sure am. Just have to decide which shoes to take."

Waving my arm around her garden, "You've done a beautiful job, Mom. It's one of the things I'm most grateful to you for — for teaching me how to garden when I was little."

"Oh . . . it saved my life so many times when your father was ill. I could come out here and dig around in the dirt for a while and then I'd feel much better. That was the best therapy for me. Now come and see my woodland garden. I just got a new fern and a really exotic hosta. They cost the earth but I couldn't resist them."

June 9th

I can't believe this is happening. Mid-flare.

Franny, Mom and I are on a plane flying to Yellowknife. We're excited and can't believe we're actually en route. The trip had been planned in February. All the details had been worked out; we were going to visit my friend Wendy and her family. Wendy is one of my oldest friends. She and I met in Nelson a few days before classes started. She was one of the people playing frisbee on the lawn the day John walked by and smiled at us all.

Then my lab tests indicated the lupus was flaring. The trip was off. Then, maybe, I wasn't flaring. The trip was on. Then, I definitely was flaring. The trip was off. I called Wendy and she said, "Don't decide now. You can change your mind right up until the day you're scheduled to come."

My medications began to do their job almost immediately and it became possible to think I could go. *But the timing won't be good. I'll be at the height of the predisone side effects. I won't be sleeping. I'll be wired.*

But then I'd begun to sleep. One little pill dissolved under my tongue took care of that.

I'd asked Dr. Bouma, "I'd like your opinion. Do you think I should go to Yellowknife?"

"If you want to and you're feeling like it, go. Your tests are showing good results. Have a good time!"

June 9th

Wendy picks us up at the airport, and the next day we drive out to Pontoon Lake, about a half hour outside of Yellowknife. Her family has three cabins on their property and there's only one other cabin on the lake. We carry all our supplies in through the sun-dappled birch forest. I'm fully protected: sunscreen, hat, long-sleeved shirt and sunglasses. We're here just a week before the longest day of the year, the summer solstice.

Twenty-four hours of daylight, possible *sun*light, and I'm not anxious.

After we settle in, we climb up the small hill behind the cabins. The birch trees are indigenous, some of the oldest ones twisted into permanent spirals by the wind. Just like the ones we'd seen in Scotland. We're walking over the flat rock of the Canadian Shield, on crunchy, greeny-yellow mosses and other plants I don't know the names of. I crouch down, bring my face as close to the ground as I can without losing focus, to the intricate web-like forms and touch them to feel their texture. Dry and hard. A scaly, celadon-coloured plant edges a black-speckled, pink and white-veined rock. Here and there, tiny wild columbines poke through clumps of moss, and clusters of delicate red berries burst through cracks in other rocks. Further on, peering down into a crevice between two huge boulders, I can see the unmistakable glint of water at the bottom, a tiny pool resting in a basin of rock. *Water.*

Wendy says just a few more weeks and there'll be thousands of tiny flowers blooming.

Wildflowers. Mauritania beads in bloom.

I begin taking micro-close photographs, shifting the camera lens and viewfinder until I find the composition I want. But I've got the prednisone "shakes" and realize the photographs will be blurred. I position the camera and Wendy takes the photographs with a steady hand. I'm humming with excitement — I'll have a new landscape to paint when I get home.

We drink tea, eat like royalty and get caught up on everything happening in our lives.

We take photographs of each other at midnight, sitting outside in full light. When I leave the cabin to go to the outhouse at three in the morning, I'm startled by the light. The openly-spaced forest reveals no wild beasts. There are bears around somewhere, but a quick scan before I head for the outhouse shows they're not around right now.

One night at around ten thirty we take the small motorboat out and go sight-seeing down the lake. A beaver swims a few feet from the boat. A bald eagle soars above us and lands on its huge nest atop a tree. We paddle into a small, shallow bay and get stuck for a few minutes.

We're sitting in a sea of green bamboo-like reeds. Now all we need for the full northwest experience is to see a bear. But we don't have our hearts set on it, really. We can go home content, I'm sure, without that experience.

The day we pack up to return to Yellowknife, Wendy and Franny load the boat with supplies and we head out down the lake to where our car is parked. They're going to drop me off, return to camp and walk out with Mom. We're a short distance from shore, Mom's waving to us and I say, "I've just left my seventy-eight-year-old mother alone in the wilds of the Northwest Territories with a dog so timid even his masters have a hard time petting him."

Franny turns to me: "I was just thinking exactly the same thing! "

It's only a few minutes; of course Mom's fine and says later, "Honestly, you two! I wasn't the least bit nervous."

~~~~

The last day we go shopping and I find a black argillite carving named "Spirit Bird" for John. It has a bird's body the size of a sparrow with a disproportionately large human head. *It looks like the prow on a Viking ship.* Cupping the carving in both of my hands, it feels cool and solid. *It has weight.* I buy a T-shirt printed with the words "soul journey" and primitive cave-painting-like figures for myself, and a different one for my friend Linda. Everything seems awash in significance. In another store, I find a banana-coloured linen skirt and decide to get it when I hear Van Morrison singing in the background on the store's music system. It must be a sign. Van thinks I should buy this skirt!

At the end of the week I fly home ahead of Mom and Franny. They're staying another four days and are going to book a guide to take them fishing, and Mom might get a round of golf in. Things I can't do because of the sun.

I arrive home exhilarated. Giddy, actually.

June 27th

Looking at my most recent test results, Dr. Bouma frowns: "Your serum creatinine has lowered to your usual level. There's no protein in your urine, but your blood complements are still too low and your sedimentation rate is still a bit high. There's enough to indicate you're not through the flare quite yet. I think we'll have to keep you on the high doses of prednisone for another month. And then we'll see."

My heart sinks. I was sure I would begin reducing the prednisone today.

I drive from the hospital down Kickwillie Loop to the lake, past the cabin, and on to Linda's where we have tea. We talk and talk and eventually I can look past the undetermined weeks of more prednisone therapy. We walk around her garden, over the thyme path, past the thatch of blue bachelor buttons to the edge of her property. Below us in the field are several cows standing beside a red barn chewing hay, their jaws moving in a side-to-side mechanical motion.

The grass is still green, the sky a benevolent grey, my friend is as she always is and the weeks will turn into days. The time will come when I can start reducing the prednisone.

June 29th

Jay arrives from Victoria to read some of his latest work. Jason will be reading, too. Jason is the publisher of Greenboathouse Books and is launching John's *Black Horses/Cobalt Suns* at Headbones Gallery on the same night.

The night of the launching I drive out to the cabin with Finnegan to see Franny and then stay behind while she goes to the reading.

~~~~

I'm sitting on the end of the pier looking out at the lake. Finnegan is a sentinel beside me — her Tibetan ancestry surfacing instinctively — watching for wayward ducks. There's a warm breeze in the air. The water is opaque and crinkly silver, like tinfoil, deep blue flickering through it. I notice a delicate spider's web spun across the top of the ladder leading to the water. The Spinner is nowhere to be seen. There aren't any bugs caught in this intricate trap. I'd have to break through its fine, iridescent web if I were to go swimming right now. It would be easy to do that. One swipe of my hand would take care of that. Another one would be spun tomorrow. But I don't break it. I leave it be, admire the complexity of its design.

I can swim tomorrow night. I'll go for my first swim of the summer then. I'll enter the water from the shore to avoid breaking the spider's web and head out for the farthest yellow buoy. No. I'll swim to the first yellow buoy. That'll be far enough.

I didn't go to John's launching because we decided it would be too emotional for both of us. John's nervous and I'm nervous for him. He could have cancelled this reading. He wanted to, but in the end goes for Jason and Jay. He doesn't want to disappoint these two former students.

Family and friends will be there. He'll be all right.

Later that night, returning from the cabin, I stop at the lake store for milk. I feel a light tap on my back and turn to see a familiar face. This person has just come from the book launch. "He was wonderful, Jude. Wonderful."

June 30th

Very bad night. Earlier in the evening we'd been out at the cabin celebrating my brother Len's birthday, and afterwards John had gone on to visit Jay and Jason at Jason's boathouse on Okanagan Lake. I'd returned home with a headache that just kept building and building — two hours of vomiting and the pressure so bad I knew at midnight this was a hospital-trip migraine.

There's no phone at the boathouse. I call Franny at the cabin. She comes right away.

John arrives at the hospital not long after we do. He'd returned home, seen the cloths and ice cubes, the Tylenol bottle, and knew where I'd be. I've had a handful of these migraines over the years, when a shot of Demerol and Gravol is the only thing that will stop the pain and nausea.

In my case, these migraines have nothing to do with lupus. I've inherited both types of headaches, migraine and tension, from my father and mother's gene pools.

The next day is rough. I'm overwhelmed by the number of pills I'm taking, the way I look, and the fact that I'll be taking high doses of prednisone for four more weeks. There's no certainty I'll be able to begin reducing the medication, even then.

I want the jitters to go away so badly. I'm tired.

I'm even tired of this euphoria. Even though it's been making the flare bearable, it isn't bringing the end of the flare any closer. Who really wants to go through life in a state of continual optimism, anyway? Who wants a one-note life? How hard would that *be to live with?*

I realize this energy and elation is purely chemical. But I also have the perception that I'm healing myself. Aside from the actual healing power of the medications which is being confirmed by my lab results, I think I'm curing the lupus with my psyche. I believe that when I come out of this flare, *I will never flare again.* The lupus will go into permanent remission. And this manuscript will show any newly diagnosed patient the way to cure themselves. *That* is going to be great.

I lived this illusion as a truth happening right then and there. For two and a half months I believed it. It was glorious. Later, when I realized it was an illusion, an artificial state of omnipotence caused by the prednisone, I eased my disappointment with the thought *I have healed myself. I've got this inner calm. This is real.*

July 2nd

OK. I'm beginnning to crash now. Before *I begin to reduce the prednisone. Have to hang on. Maybe only three more weeks of high-dose steroids. My eyes are tired. They feel gritty and dry. Blurry too. Even my sight is jittery. Must be the prednisone.*

Was it like this for you, Dad? The crash into depression after the manic phase of your illness. Did you miss the highs when you were leveled by the lows? Did it all seem too much for you at times? I wish I could talk to you. You are here, though. I can feel you here.

I can't see beyond all this. I just want to go to sleep and have someone wake me up when it's all over. When I'm better.

July 10th

I'm still calm inside. That hasn't gone away. I think about little Christopher and wonder how he's doing. I think about his braveness and his patience. I don't want to call the school because I'm afraid someone will tell me he isn't doing well. I don't call.

July 12th to 18th

I'm no longer writing. I'm way, way down. Not in Jennifer Warne's "glory" place. I'm somewhere the opposite of that. I can't bring myself up.

Sometimes I hide from you. Go to a dark cave somewhere and crawl inside. I don't want you to find me. I can't bear your worry. I can't bear that you have to live this life. Sometimes I think I could be brave and let you go. Tell you to go to a life that's less painful. But I'm not that brave. I love you too much. Can you forgive me this?

John still plays and practises with Neil and Shelby on the weekends, but rarely goes out socially on his own. He doesn't want to have to explain why I'm not there or even to have to tell people I'm still sick. Three or four months into a kidney flare, someone will ask him, "Is she feeling better now?" And three months later, they're startled when he tells them that I'm still sick or still recovering.

Is anybody asking John how he is? I doubt he's being truthful, if they are. Can I even really know what these flares are like for him?

We move through these days mechanically now. We're professionals. We've been here before and we know what to do. We're more careful than usual with one another, knowing our nerves are frayed, our resources depleted, knowing how easily a word, said in a certain tone of voice, could hurt the other. Sometimes we do lose our balance and lash out, say things to one another that we immediately regret and apologize for. *Wolf is saying, "You are forgiven." I'm* saying, "We can't even fight like a normal couple when I'm in a flare. Are we to be spared nothing?"

We rely wearily on our love for one another.

I'm counting the days until we leave for Vancouver and I can see Dr. Penn. Linda arrives one day and I break down as soon as I see her. My hands and legs are shaking.

My whole body is vibrating. She puts her arms around me and says, "Oh, Jude, you're about to pop. They've got to get you off these drugs." Then Franny comes through the kitchen door smiling. As soon as she sees me, her face crumples. She crosses over and puts her arms around me.

July 19th

It's four in the morning. John and I are loading up my mother's car, loaned for the trip to Vancouver because of it's air conditioning. We want to beat the sun. I've packed the cooler with sandwiches, strawberries and blueberries and drinking water. I sleep the trip away. We've got a room waiting for us at the Sylvia Hotel in English Bay and a 5:30 p.m. appointment with Dr. Penn.

July 19th, 6:00 p.m.

Ushering me into his office, Dr. Penn says, "I'm sorry you're flaring again."

His office is in the heart of Vancouver, close to a teaching hospital. He has a view of other high buildings from his office window. I can hear the muffled tones of rush-hour traffic through its pane.

Sitting now, I say, "I've been trying to figure out what triggered it."

Dr. Penn puts his pen down and sits back in his chair. His manner is alert and attentive. When he speaks, it is directly and simply, an approach I find calming. In doctors' offices my brain always imagines the worst possible scenario. (Like the kind Woody Allen portrays so hilariously in his movies, except that it's not so funny in Real Life.) The phrase "can happen" instantly translates to "will happen" in my mind. I can hear the hiss of "fatal outcome" in any tone of voice.

Dr. Penn always makes me feel comfortable enough to speak my anxieties. Because of this, he can correct information I've misconstrued before I leave his office. And by listening attentively to my firsthand experience of lupus, he makes me feel like an intelligent human being whose observations are important to his own knowledge of the disease.

He says now, "There isn't always a reason. It just happens with lupus."

I lean forward in my chair. "But there is something. At the end of April, I had immunization shots for meningitis and hepatitis. My GP recommended I have the vaccines but I put off getting them for five months. Something in my gut was telling me not to. But I did, finally. I'm always such a damn good patient. A month later my blood tests started acting up. I never flare in the spring. You had called me in January just to tell me I was in good health, asymptomatic, and to keep doing whatever it was I was doing to stay healthy."

"There is the likelihood those shots triggered the lupus."

My body clenches, *If I hadn't had the shots, I might not have flared. I wouldn't be in this hell of a flare.* Then relief replaces the anger because John and I had been hoping the vaccines were responsible for the flare. This would mean it was an aberration. But it's not that simple. We can't know, unequivocally, that the vaccines caused my immune system to turn on itself, attacking my kidneys.

Now I'm sitting on the edge of my seat. "So this flare *could* be an aberration and I may not have flared again for my usual five or even seven years."

"It's possible." Then he lifts both hands in a "we just don't know" kind of gesture. "If you had called me, I would have recommended those shots. I recommend them to all my patients with kidney-involved lupus."

I tell him what my initial reaction was. Passing his hand over his neatly-cut dark beard, he responds, "I can understand your anger and appreciate your relief." While he's jotting something down in my file, I look out the window at the early evening light. *Vancouver is such a beautiful city.*

I still really want it to be the vaccinations. My heart is insisting it be so. I turn back to Dr. Penn, "But this *could* be an example of a rare occurrence, in that the lupus was triggered by the vaccine serum? I *could* be the one person out of a zillion or whatever, that had a negative reaction to the vaccine?"

He stops writing and lifts his head. "Yes."

"So this isn't *It?* The end of the road. It doesn't necessarily mean the kidney disease has reached the point where the flares will come closer together and be more severe until I reach end-stage kidney failure?"

With emphasis: "Jude, you're not anywhere near there. We're not even thinking about that, much less talking about it. So put that out of your mind. You're asymptomatic. You're in remission."

~~~~

We're in the examining room now. Dr. Penn's taken my blood pressure, pressed my ankles for swelling and we've been discussing restaurants in Vancouver where you can get good take-out.

Now he's rinsing his hands at the sink. "Your blood pressure is fine." And then he says the magic words, "You can begin reducing the prednisone now. In two weeks, cut down to 50 mg a day."

In two weeks.

Turning round, he sees my expression and says, "No, you can reduce it to 50 mg today. In two weeks, reduce it again to 40 mg and so on until you're back to your maintenance dose of 15 mg every second day."

"Thank you."

Back in his office we discuss my new pill regime combining cyclophosphimide and azathioprine with a small dose of prednisone. He explains the side effects of oral versus intravenous cyclophosphimide therapy. There's no debate here. Dr. Penn makes it perfectly clear oral is the way to go: "I would never put you on intravenous cyclophosphimide when you're in remission anyway."

Later, at the hotel, we phone Franny and ask her to let Mom know how the appointment went too. We leave the hotel and walk down the busy street looking for a place to have dinner. Reading menus propped by doors, we choose the Brass Monkey. We sit at an outside table facing the street where we can watch the people streaming by. We've been sitting at tables like this one for twenty-five years now. Talking and laughing. Tonight we're remembering the excitement of our first time together in Vancouver twenty-four years ago.

After dinner we cross the street to the Bread Garden, choose a sumptuous dessert, take it back to the beach and find a log to sit on. We watch all the people strolling, running, skateboarding, roller-blading and bicycling by. As dusk falls, lights begin appearing across the water on the other side of the bay and boat-lights bob and speckle the water in the deepening blue of nightfall.

I dig the toes of my shoes into the sand. "This is nice."

John puts his arm around me and says, looking out at the water, "This is really nice."

~~~~

The next morning we have breakfast in the hotel, pack up and begin the trip home. Arriving at a rest stop in Meritt around noon, we stop for refreshments. When I step out of the air-conditioned car, a wave of heat washes over me. There isn't a blade of green grass or a tree anywhere to be seen. All around me people are smiling, joking and delighting in the summer day. They all look incredibly healthy. They're wearing sandals, shorts, sleeveless tops. Their exposed skin is tanned.

Returning from the washroom, I glance down at my bruised, white legs showing beneath my cotton skirt, lift one foot after the other and pull myself through the thick air towards the car.

John's there, leaning against the car's hood. *At least he looks hot, too.* We climb back into the car. I rearrange the towels to cover the window on my side, and safely shaded, cooled again by the airconditioning, we head back out to the highway.

"You know, Jude, the heat's too much for me and I'm not allergic to the sun. And all those healthy, tanned bodies you were looking at back there are the bodies of twenty-year-old kids. You looked like that when you were twenty, too. Did you notice the people our age? They were all wilting."

True.

July 26th

"It seems like the final cruelty, you know. I have a great life. Even with all of this I have a great life and I'm so grateful for that . . . but . . . it's so overwhelming at times. What the prednisone does to my face. I don't even recognize myself in the mirror. I don't want to leave the house anymore. I'm in remission and I'm so tired and feel so defeated. And I'm afraid of this new drug, cyclophosphimide."

Tears are streaming down my cheeks. I'm not looking at Dr. Bouma. He reaches out a hand across the desk; I take it, cry even more at this kindness and eventually begin to calm down.

"Do your tests every month now instead of every two weeks and at our next appointment we'll sit down together and read about cyclophosphimide. Book a thirty-minute appointment so we'll have enough time."

Together. This is the word that saves me. When I return home, I find my new prescription bottle and swallow a cyclophosphimide pill with two large glasses of water. Dr. Penn had told me I must drink between two and three litres of liquid daily, to avoid the negative side effects of the medication.

The Wolf can do this. She can fill her belly with water. She's a Cancer so water is her sign. (Actually, she was born on the cusp of Cancer and Leo, which explains why she is mostly a "nester", but given the right circumstance and mood, also likes to go out into the world.) Surely she can drink the vast amounts required, knowing how good it is for her body.

Three Days Later

I wonder what the cyclophosphimide is doing? It's too soon for side effects. I doubt if it's doing anything yet. You don't take three pills and boom, strange things start happening to your body. Just let it be, for now.

I let it be.

July 29th

Despairingly, I say, "Honestly, Franny. Look at me!"

"What?" she asks, as she curls her legs under her on the couch, getting comfortable.

I point to my face. "My eyes are slits between puffy lids and one eye is continually dripping. My neck is as thick as a wrestler's. Never mind a double chin. I've got a quadruple one. I'm an official member of "The Club of Chins" now: Jay Leno, Brian Mulroney and *moi*. The Firm of Wobble: Leno, Mulroney and Clarke."

Now we're starting to laugh.

"And in this heat it feels like my chin is stuck to my neck with velcro!" I demonstrate by lifting my chin and it sticks, stretches a little before releasing from my neck. I get up and adjust the venetian blind, closing out the sun, and continue, "My cheeks are so bloated they're pulling my whole face downwards. My mouth is creased into a permanent frown."

Flopping back down on the couch, I continue, "I had to go into the Motor Vehicle office the other day and renew my driver's licence. The woman helping me said, 'I have to take your picture or I can't give you a licence. Look,' she says, 'when you smile, it lifts your face and it doesn't look as bad.'"

"She actually said that?"

"Yes, she did. So I guess I should go around smiling all the time. How about this?" I contort my face into a forced toothy grimace which makes us both laugh more.

"And I've got this mustache that's growing longer and darker by the week. Pretty soon I'm going to be able to comb it or wax it and I'll be Salvador Dali! But, and this is a good thing, when it's safe, I'll go and have it removed by electrolysis. The hair is superficial, easily pulled and doesn't grow back."

"Really?" says Franny. "Let me know when you're going because I've got a few chin hairs I'd like to get rid of."

"Gawd, so do I." I mime drawing three long strands of chin hair together, crossing them over and under into a braid which ends in my lap. This gets us howling and holding our stomachs. "And my hair! All this damp weather is totally frizzing it out. When I asked John the other day which of the Three Stooges I was thinking I looked like, without a second's hesitation, he said, 'Larry!'"

Tears are running down our cheeks now, we're laughing so hard. I splutter out, "Apparently, according to the literature, people with lupus generally have thin, sparse hair!" I put my hand under my mop of thick, curly hair, lift and dramatically flip it out.

August 10th

I begin to feel better about the new treatment. I've had time to think about my appointment in Vancouver with Dr. Penn. Even though I now have a whole new raft of questions, I'm reassured knowing I'll be able to get the answers to them at my next appointment with Dr. Bouma.

I forget my bloated face.

~~~~

The Wolf snarls and moves in, sinks his teeth into my wrist, begins dragging me over that airless grey landscape again. It's that other Wolf, the one who weighs me down when I reduce the prednisone to a certain point, drags my body through each day. He's right on schedule and he's no less ruthless than he's been in all the other flares.

~~~~

The prednisone has sucked all the energy — artificial and real — out of me. My brain is tired. I force myself out of bed in the morning, look around at our messy house and think *I'm back.* I start to vacuum the hall. Soon, I have to lie down on the couch, nauseous, out of breath. I wait for the nausia to pass, my heartbeat to steady, then get up and head for the computer. *Writing is quiet. It's been a good thing for this flare. Another surprise.*

My spirits are good for a day, then down for several, then good days alternate with bad. After several weeks of this, the Wolf loosens his grip a little. Once or twice throughout these good-spirit days, I'm aware I'm not as exhausted. There are moments now when my brain feels clear. I have glimpses of my real self. Then I have four good days in a row. *It's beginning to happen now.*

August

Over two hundred forest fires are burning in B.C. right now. We've had unrelentingly hot weather for over two weeks. The largest fire is burning just south of the Merrit rest stop we pulled into on our way home from Vancouver last month. It's over 380 hectares. We can smell the smoke in the air here in Vernon, and see it too. Especially at the lake. At dusk, the hills are an eerie red and Kalamalka a bowl of still grey smoke. I don't swim in it.

All around the province wildfire is blazing its way across meadows and through forests. Men and women are out there fighting down the flames. Foot soldiers. Helicopters are dropping chemicals. Chemical warfare. That's how you treat it. Aggressively. There will be consequences to using the chemicals, unwanted side effects, but in the end the fires will be contained and the forests and meadows will begin to grow again, to turn green.

One fire is put out. Another catches and blazes out of control. Another is put out. Gain ground, lose ground. That's how it goes.

It's the pattern of wildfire.

Here in the Okanagan, we live with it. We find ways to cope. Sometimes we're successful and sometimes we're not. But we would never just leave the blaze to run rampant. We pay attention, and paying attention is what makes it a little more likely that the fires will eventually die down or not get too far out of control in the first place.

The earth, air, and water will eventually cool down again. So will this body and this soul.

August 30th

"How are you feeling?"
   "Better, emotionally, than the last time you saw me."
   "Good. How about physically?"
   "Just fine."
   Dr. Bouma looks up from my file and frowns. "Jude, your serum creatinine level is up a little again. Don't reduce the prednisone any more until we see what's going on here. Your blood pressure is very good. I'll write you a requisition and you can do your tests again, right after this appointment. I'm sorry to give you this news."
   He stands up and goes over to a bookcase, pulls out a huge book, sits down again and begins leafing through it. When he finds what he's looking for, he reads out loud the possible side effects of cyclophosphimide. I can't concentrate. *I can't feel my heart beating.* I'm not prepared for what he has just told me. *I'm in remission. I've been asymptomatic for a few weeks. What's going on? This has never happened before. A relapse? Because of the changes in my medication? Something else? Nobody can answer these questions.*

~~~~

Two weeks later, my lab results are back where they should be.

March, 2001

It's midnight at the Golden Horseshoe, a small café in Armstrong. The place is packed, people standing at the bar and at the back. The Trio is winding down the night. By now, the audience is "frisky" as John would say, and calling out, responding to John's humour which is most often at either Neil or Shelby's or his own expense. If you're a friend in the audience, you don't want to draw attention to yourself when John's around, because he's sure to include you in the fun.

There are several people dancing (all women, of course) which is remarkable because there isn't a dance floor. They're about two feet from the band. The trio is doing Bob Dylan's "Watchtower". Shelby and Neil are playing their guitars like there's no tomorrow and John's singing, giving it up, giving it all up for the crowd. Rhonda and I join the dancers. John raises an eyebrow at me. I raise one back.

I love the feel of this. I love the feel of everything tonight.

Now everyone is seated again and the Trio is playing their last song for the night, a slow country western melody John wrote called "The Real World". John begins singing and on the chorus, Shelby and Neil lift their heads to their voice microphones and join him.

In the morning when the birds rise up
And their song becomes the world
And my feet move down through the house
And the day starts to unfurl

I get the coffee going
Then I wake you with a smile
And we sit talking for a while

And I know this is the real world
We dream it all the time
I know this is the real world
We cannot seem to find

Why do we turn our backs on it
As if it wasn't there
When we're standing all around it
In the air

In the evening when the sun slips through
The edges of those hills
And all the night sounds chatter
While the street becomes so still

And we walk out in the garden
To see what we have grown
And whisper beneath the quarter moon

And I know this is the real world
We dream it all the time
I know this is the real world
We cannot seem to find

Why do we turn our backs on it
As if it wasn't there
When we're standing all around it
In the air

~~~~

At the age of twenty-one, I would have given anything to be able to see into my future. Of course, I only wanted to see one thing: my survival. *No, that's not true.* I wanted to see an exceptional life, too — one full of love and art — and I wanted to live that life with John. *So did you get this? Yes. And more.* You hear often from people who have experienced life-threatening illness that facing their own mortality has given them the ability to appreciate and love what their life *is.* It's all true what we say.

I remember clearly that first odd but seemingly insignificant sign which forebode the beginning of a lifetime of coping with lupus for me.

I see that seventeen-year-old girl smoking a cigarette with her friends in a car on a winter night in a small town in the interior of B.C. The girl observes with casual curiosity her finger turn white in the cold and then blue when she warms it under her armpit. Two years after that, she spends a whole summer in the blazing sun, hiking up and down a mountain all day, tree planting. She's the strongest she's ever been. She's thin, but all muscle, and tanned a dark brown, as she always is at summer's end. She has no way of knowing there is an ember glowing deep within her body and that soon it will burst into flame, or that this is the last summer she will feel truly invincible; that this is the last summer for many things and the first summer for many others.

All the years since I was diagnosed, I think I've been trying to catch the rhythm of the disease. It's like when I paint. It's a natural process for me to feel the rhythm of a composition, trust my instincts and go with it. A willingness to improvise is the key here. Some days I don't find the rhythm, but I've learned not to keep on trying.

Invariably, I overwork the painting if I keep on. I know, now, when to leave well enough alone.

I think this has always been part of my struggle with lupus; I wanted to find the rhythm of the disease and it seemed the harder I tried, the more self-conscious I was about it, the more it eluded me. I should have known that. My most successful paintings are always the unselfconscious ones. It's been waiting for me all this time. I just had to feel it.

I've found the rhythm. It's an improvisation. I can feel it.

~~~~

The Wolf is swimming now, gliding through the cool water, a warm body moving through a fluid landscape in the evening light. The water is a balm against her skin — the lake, a delicious kind of sanctuary. All around her are golden hills quilted with summer-green orchards, and beyond these great, forested, blue mountains. The only sound in her ears is the quiet intake and release of her own breathing, the steady beating of her heart.

JUDE CLARKE